# Koala Coloring Book For Adults

***This Coloring book belongs to:***

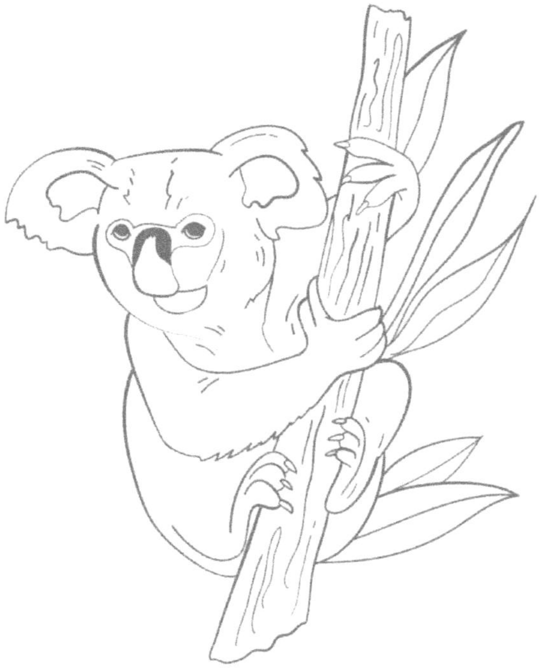

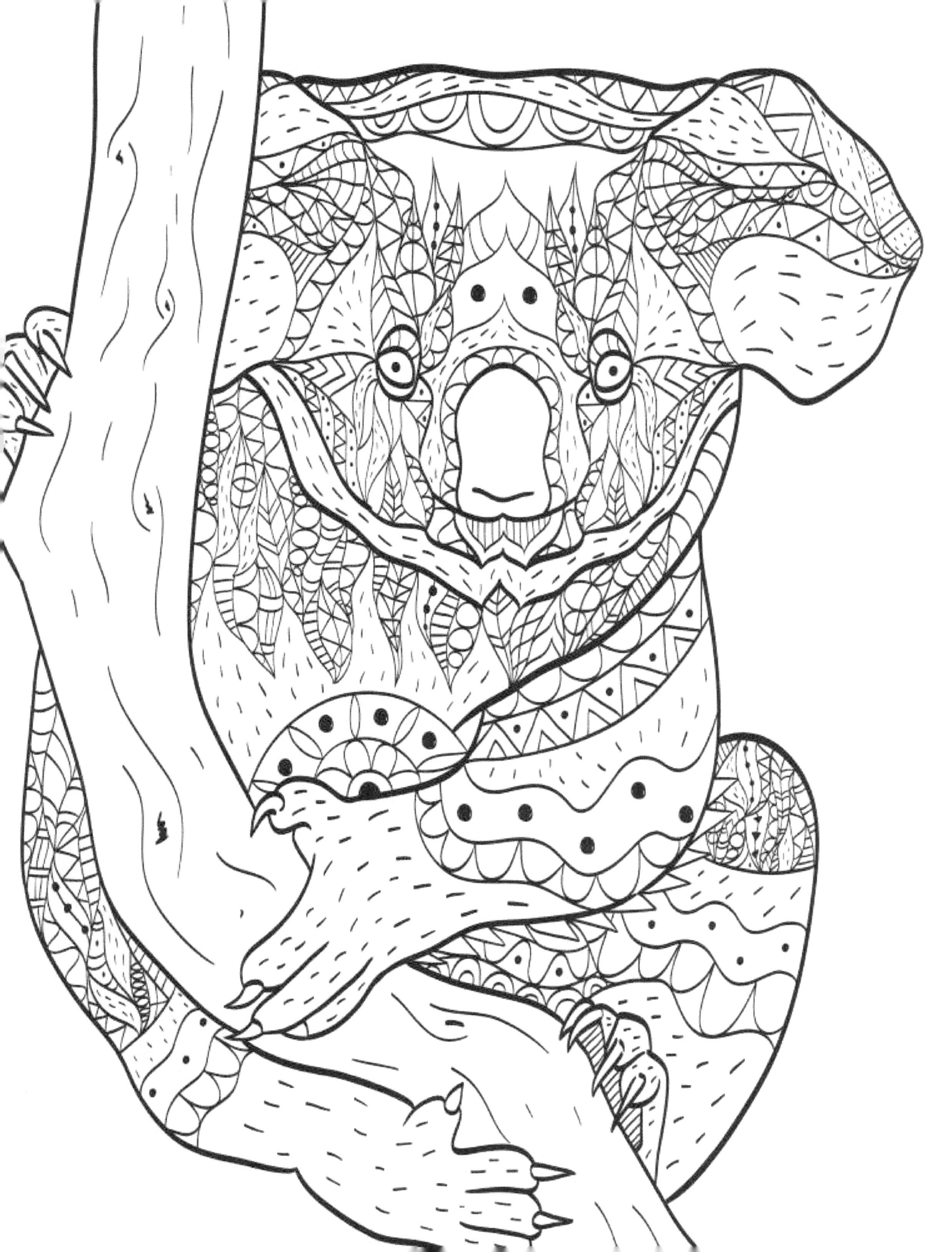

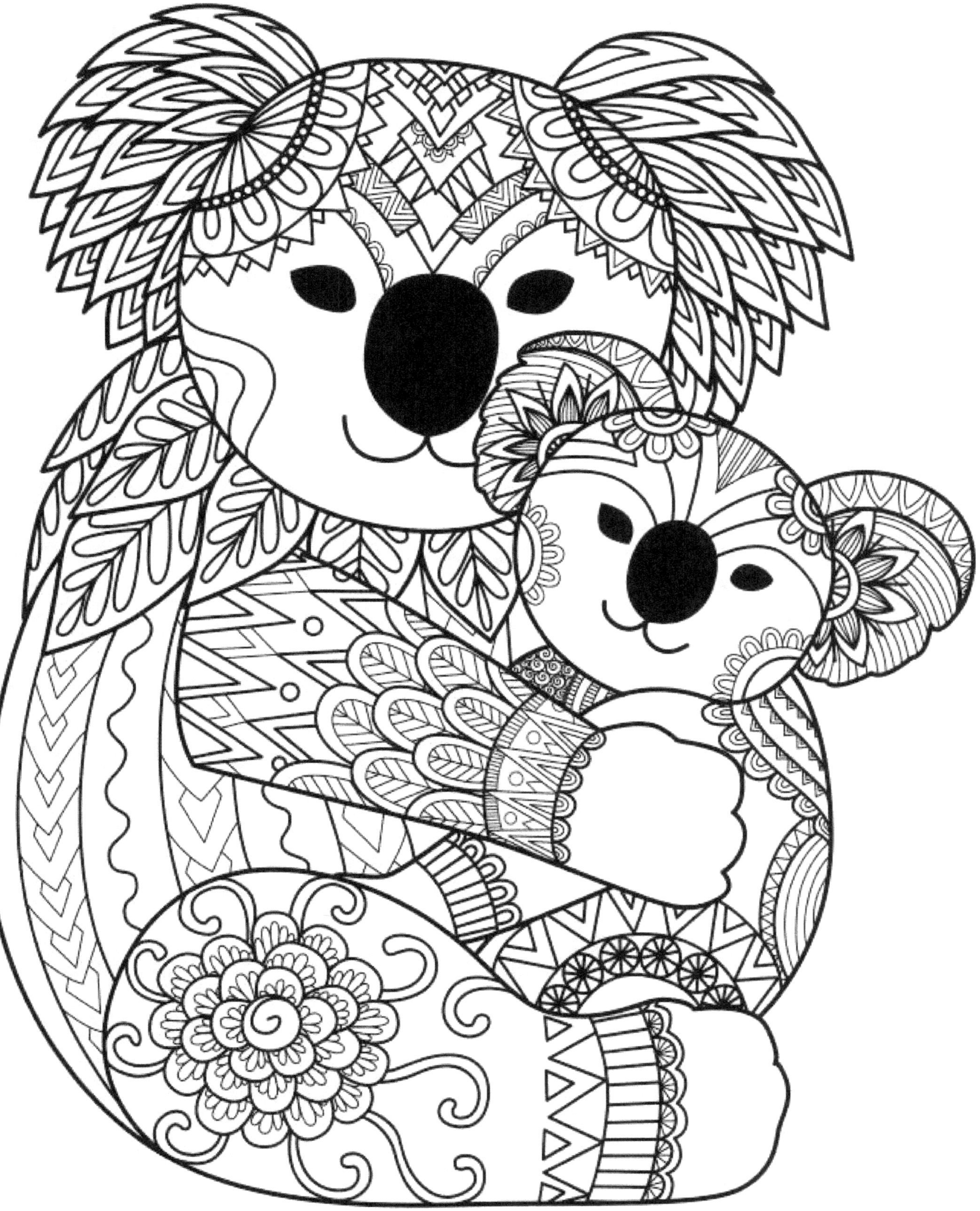

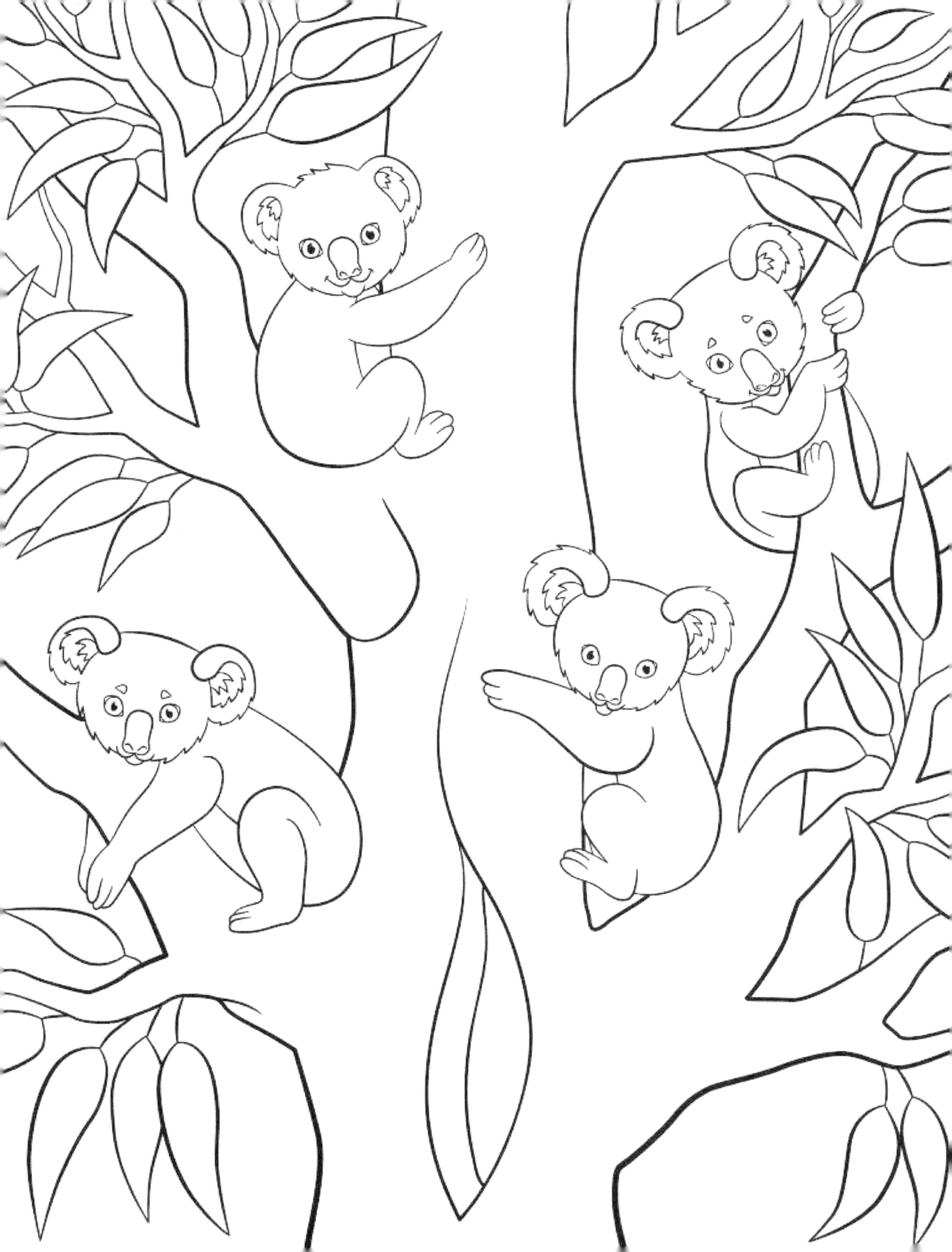

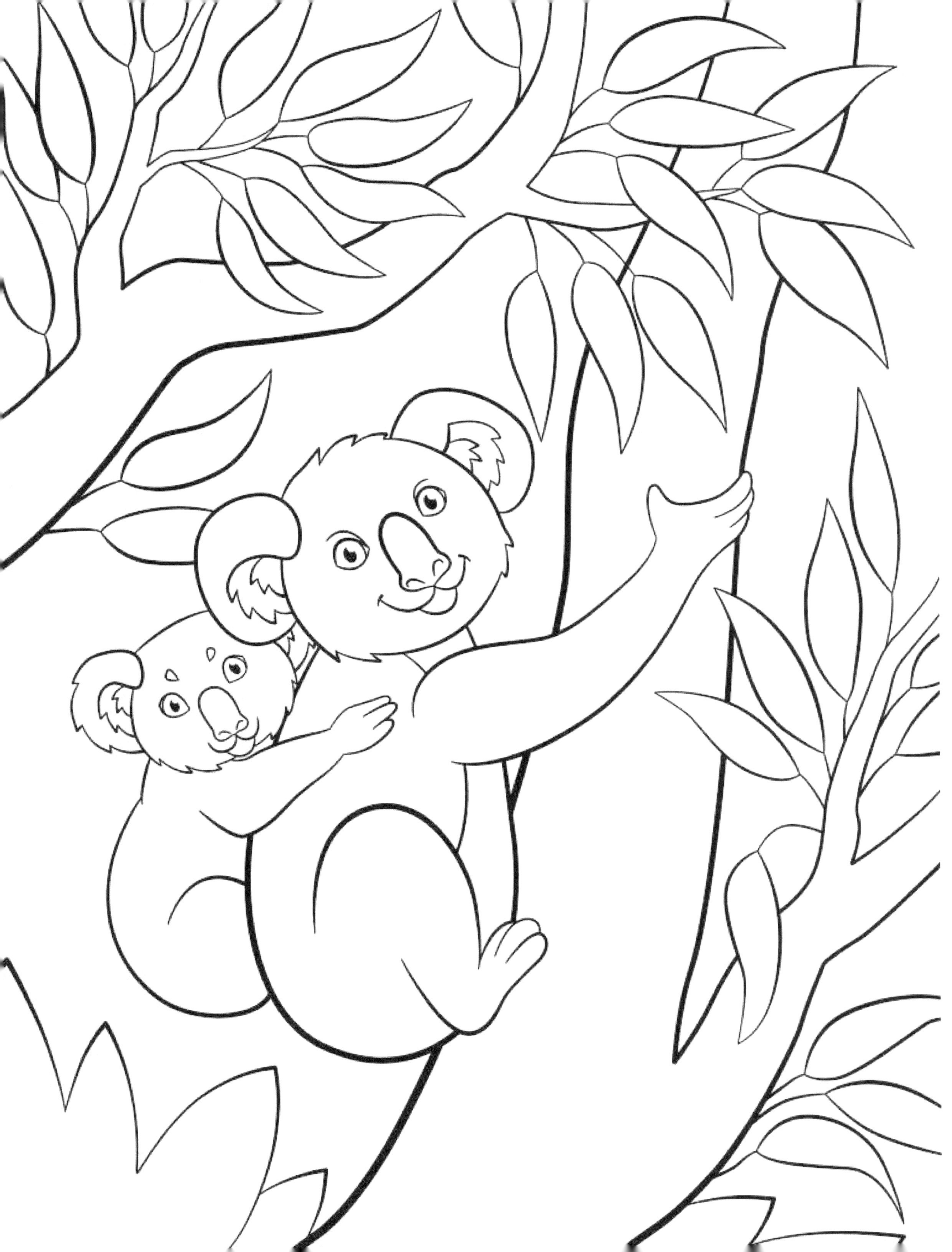

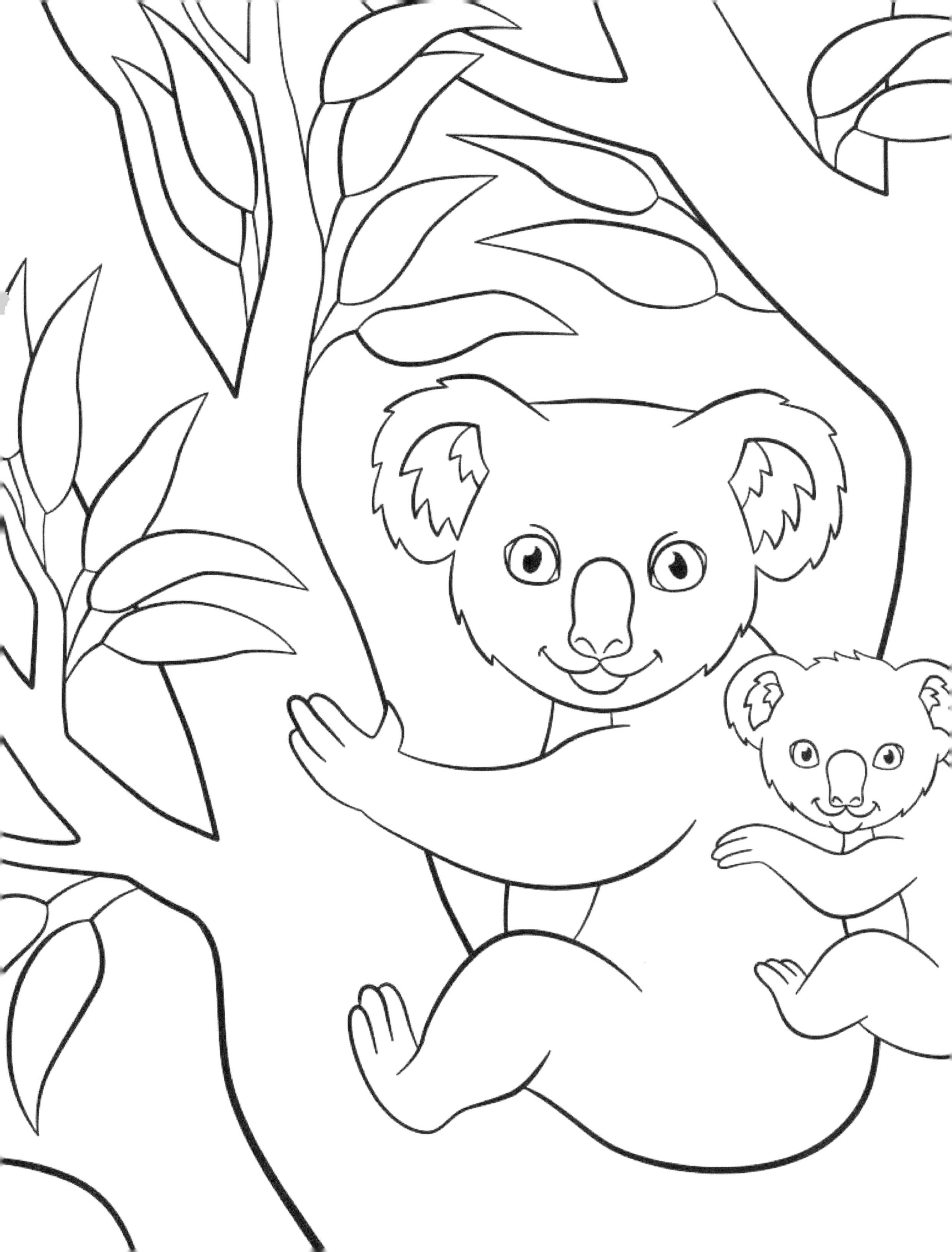

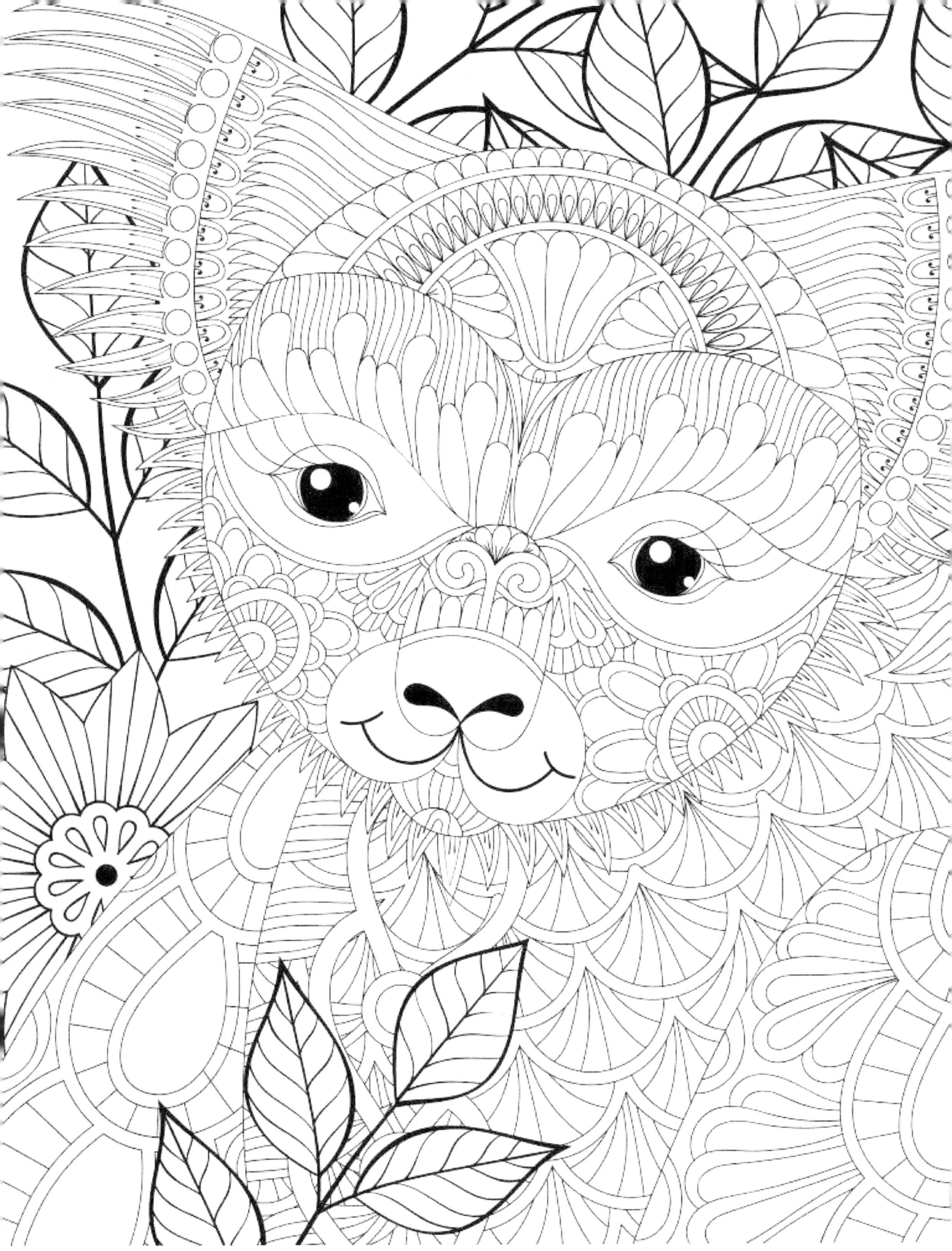

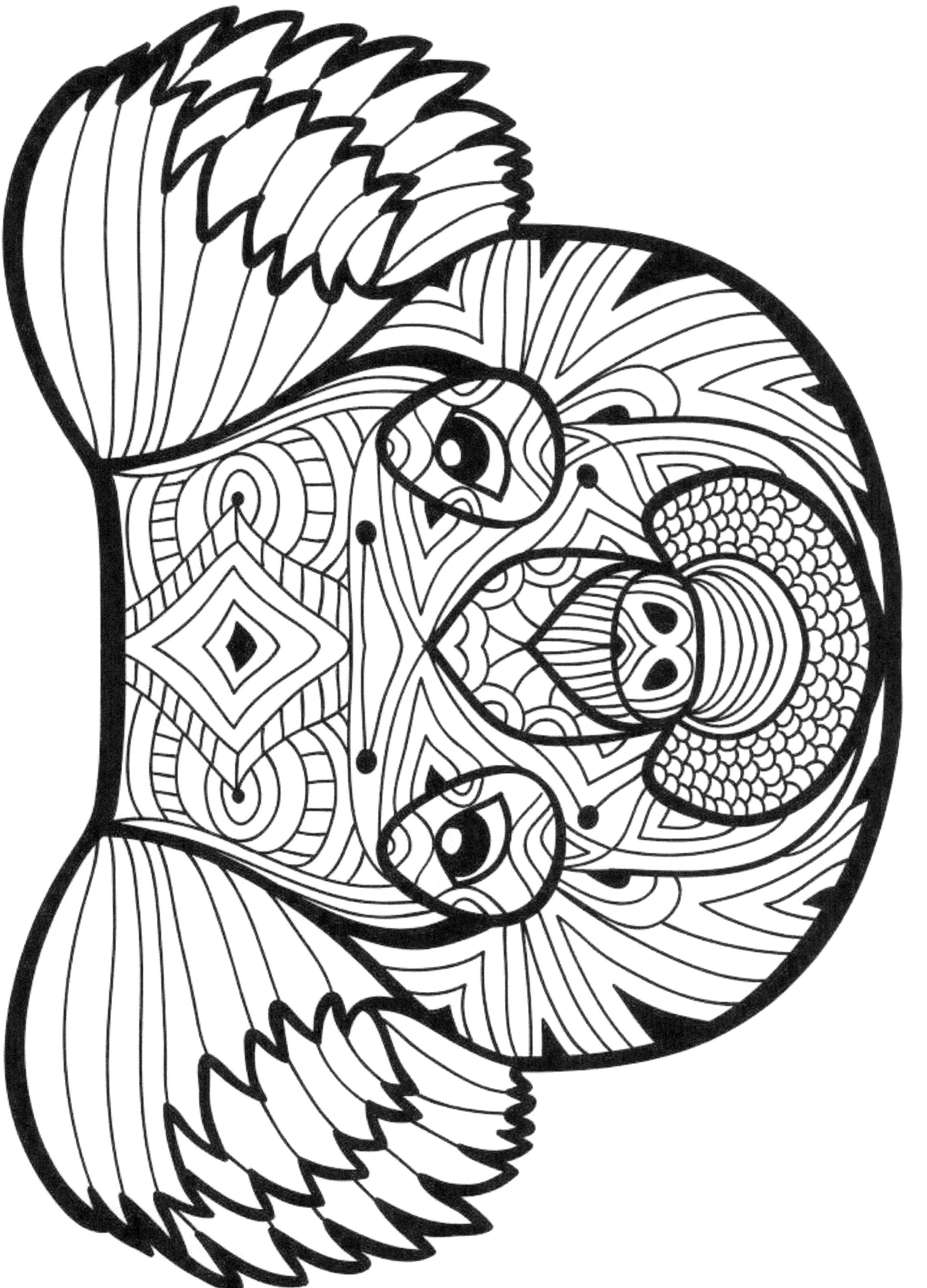

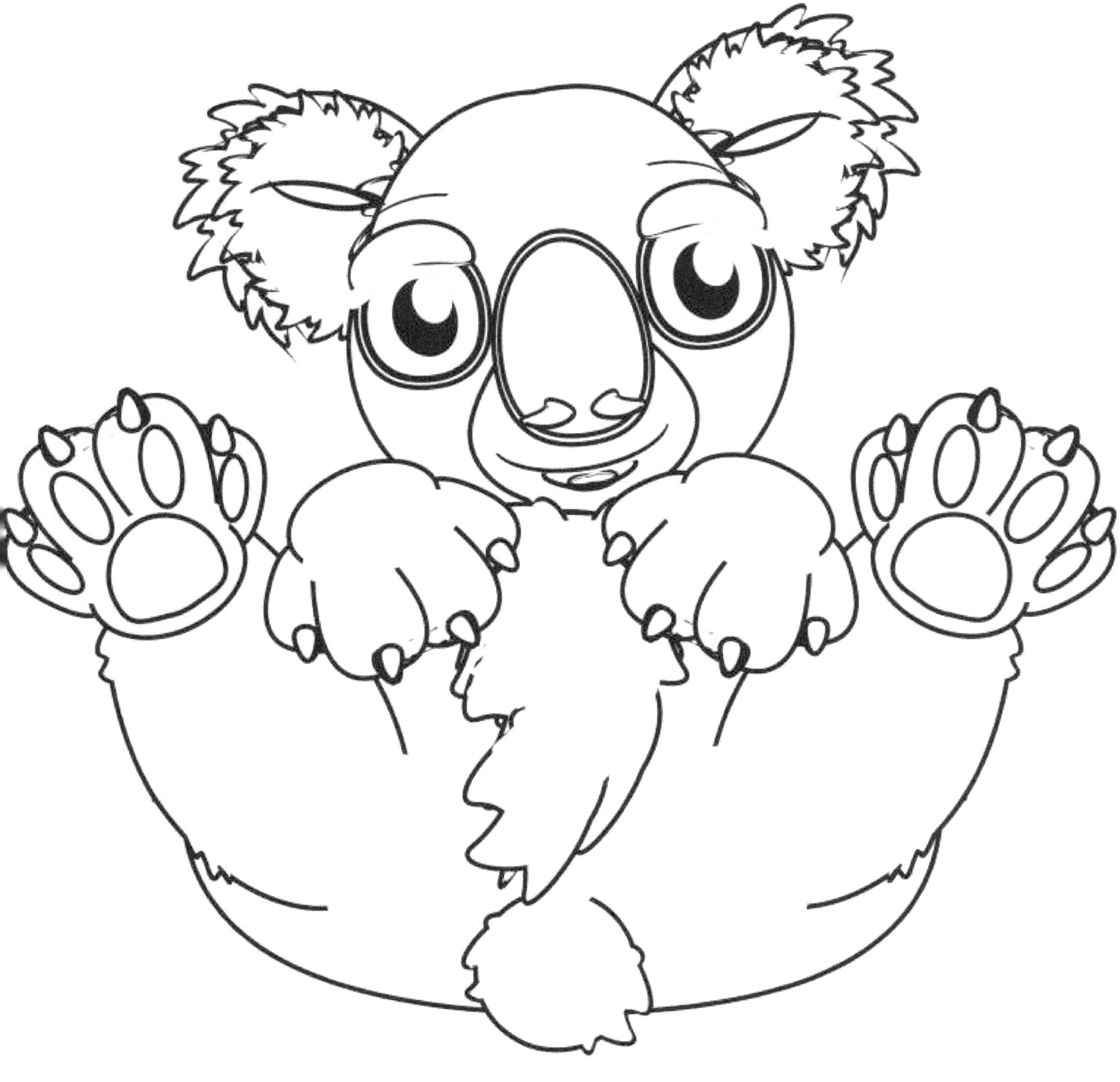

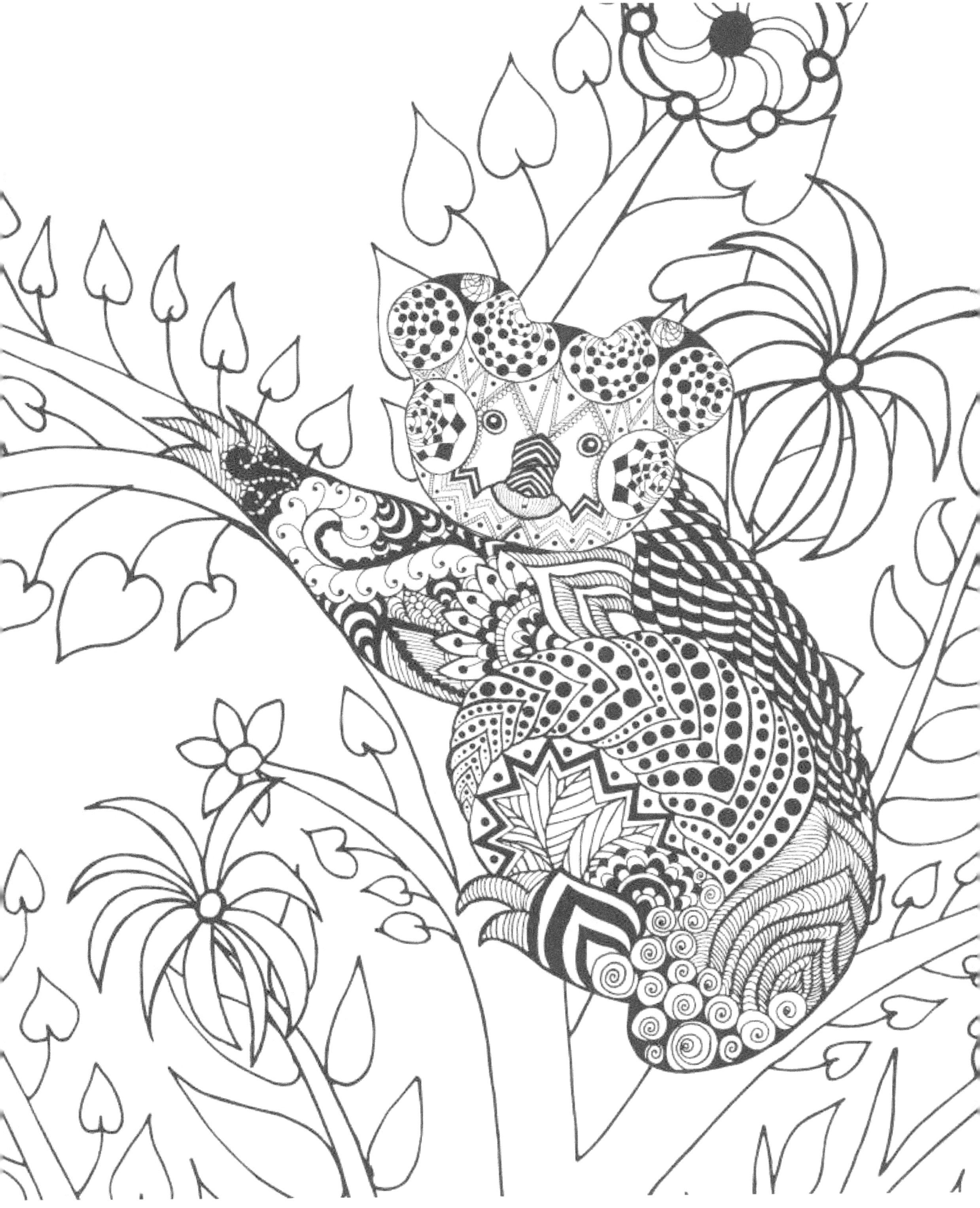

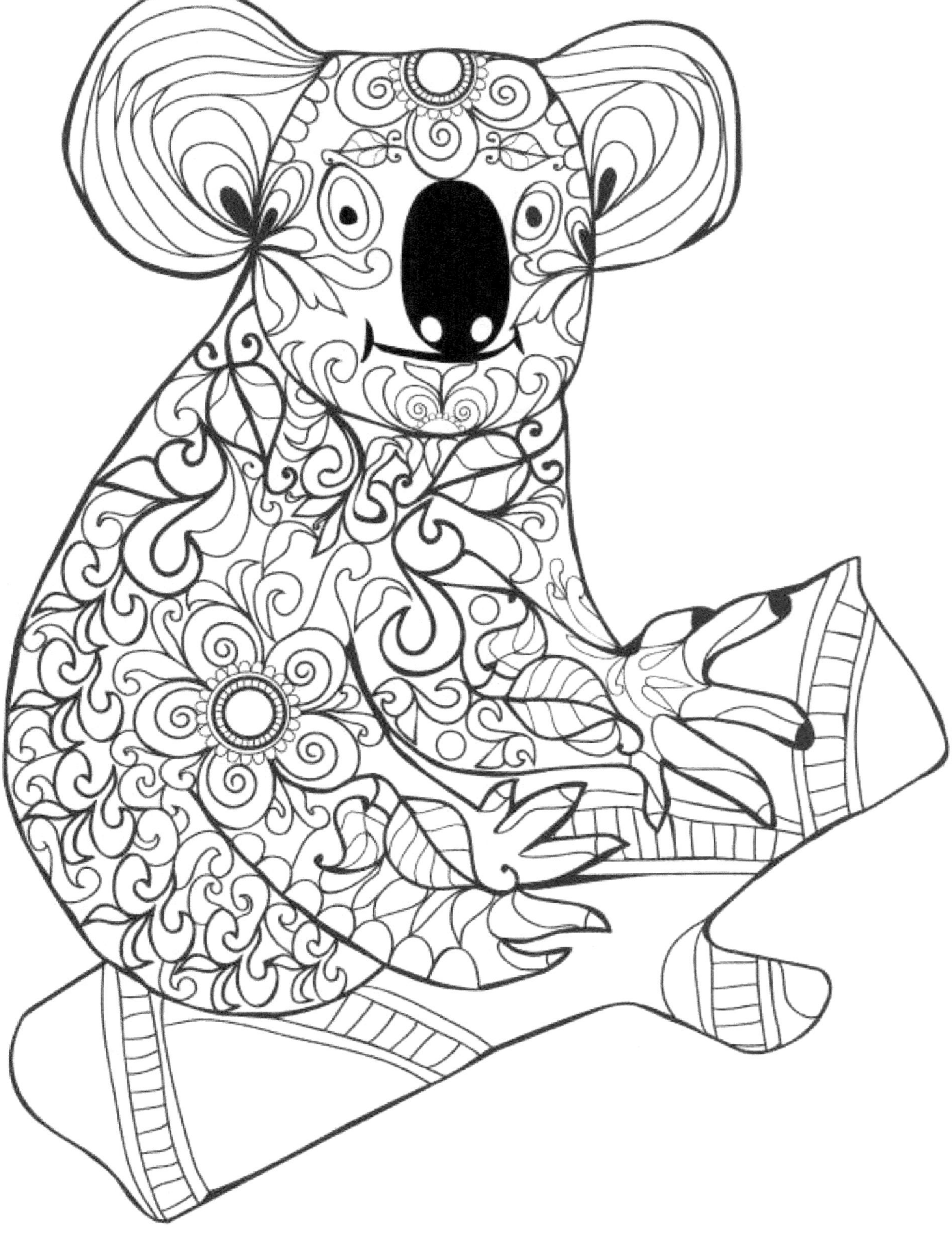

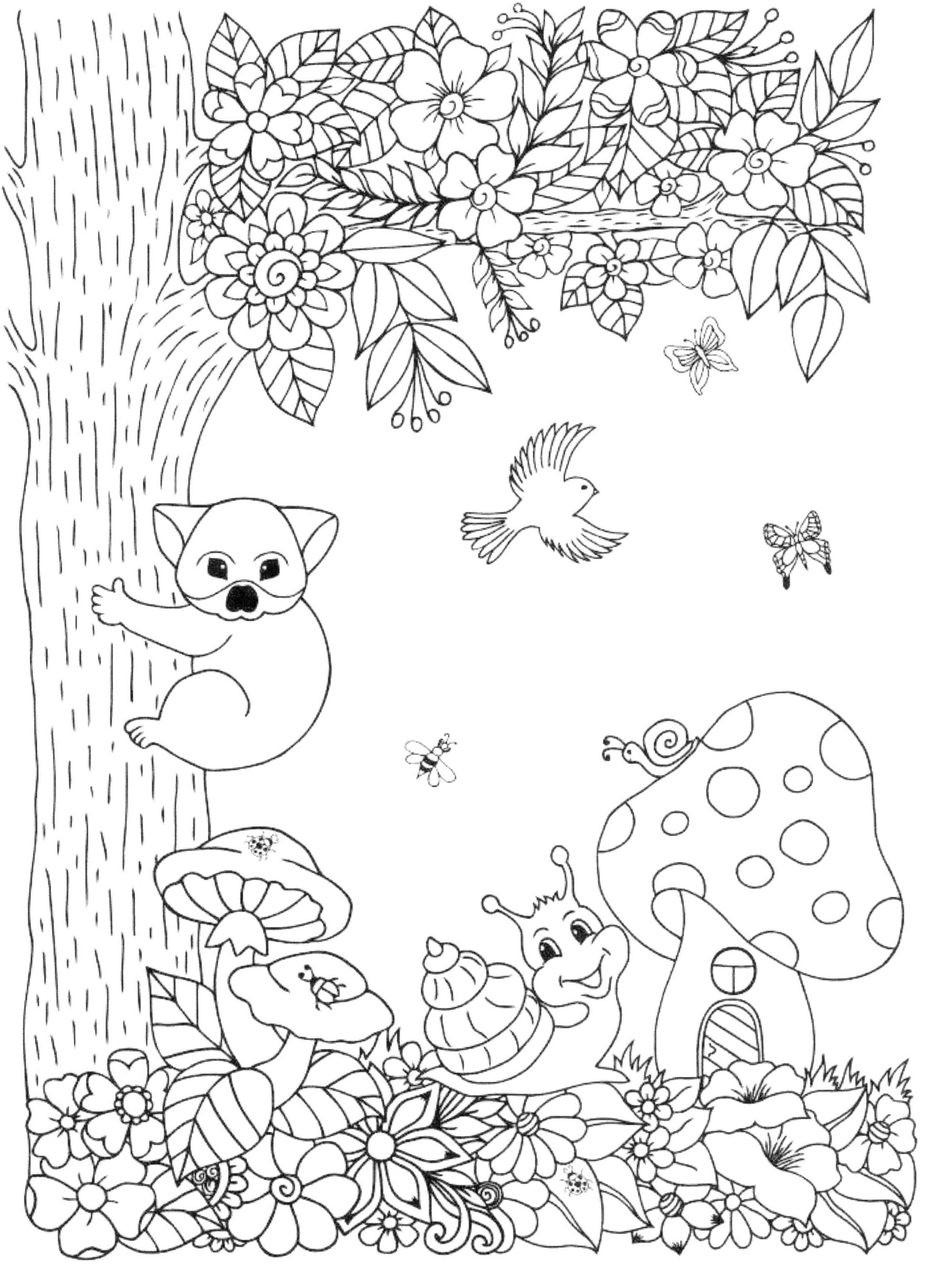

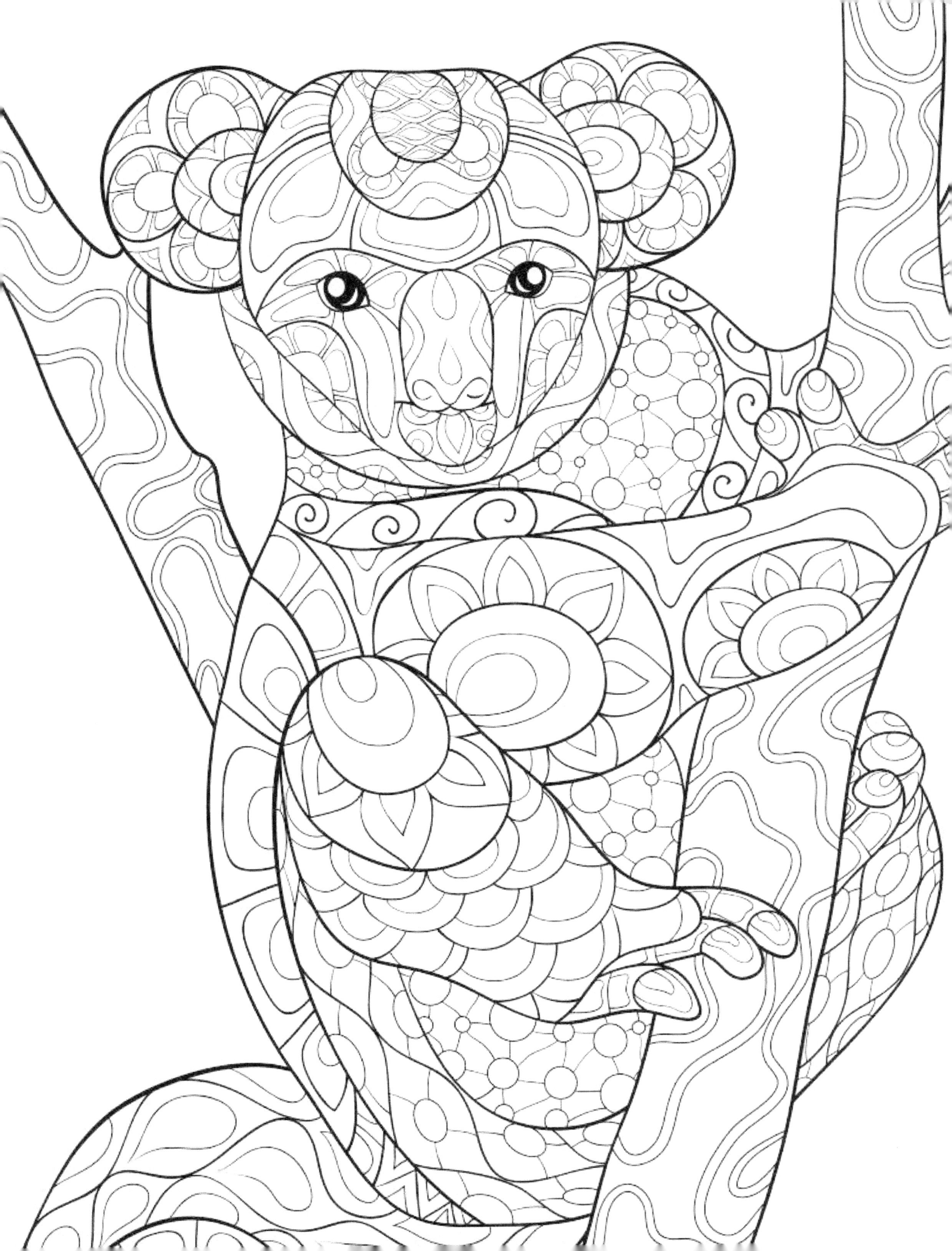

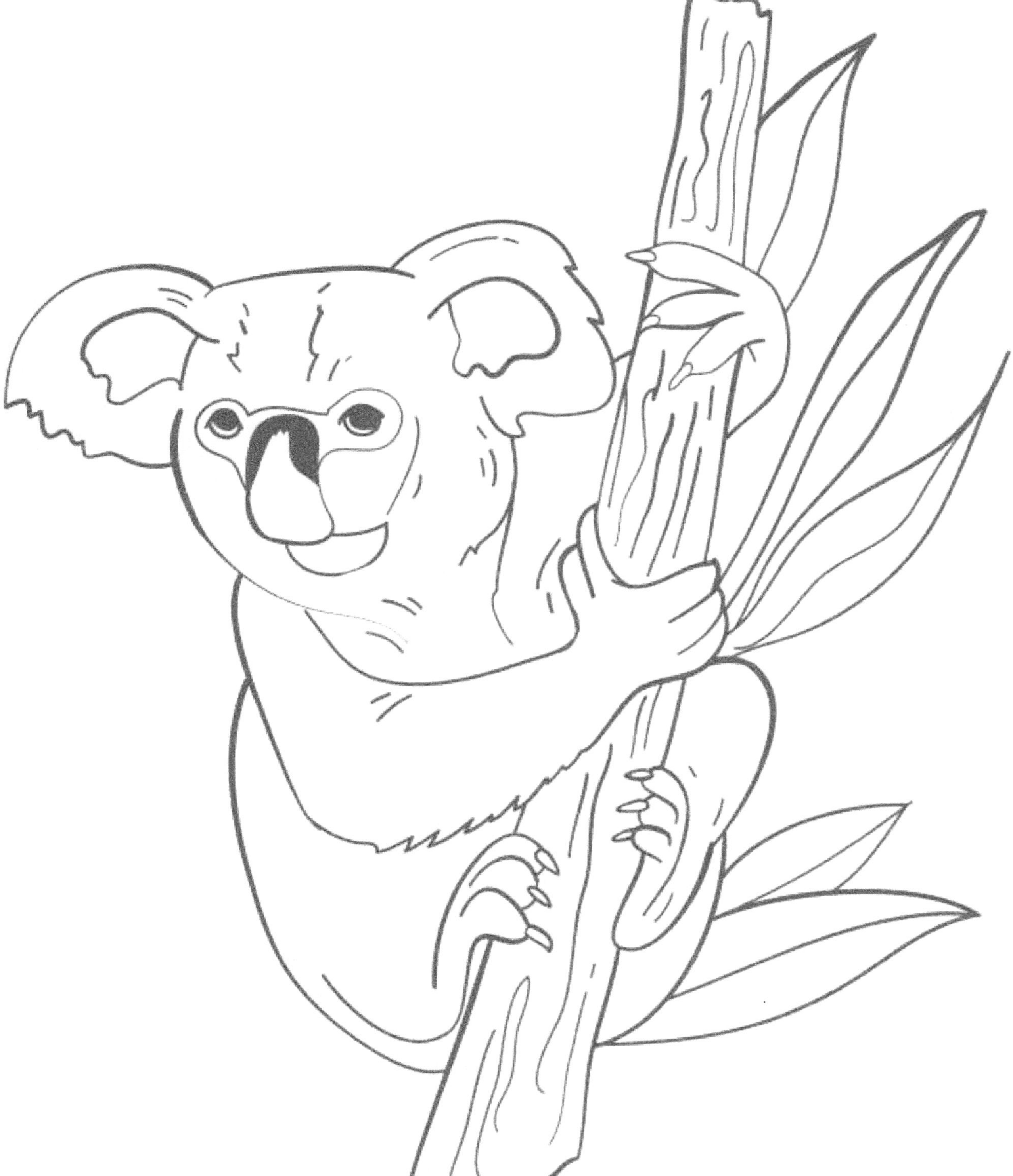

**Surprise Bonus Cute Dogs and Beautiful Sea Turtles Coloring Pages. Enjoy!**

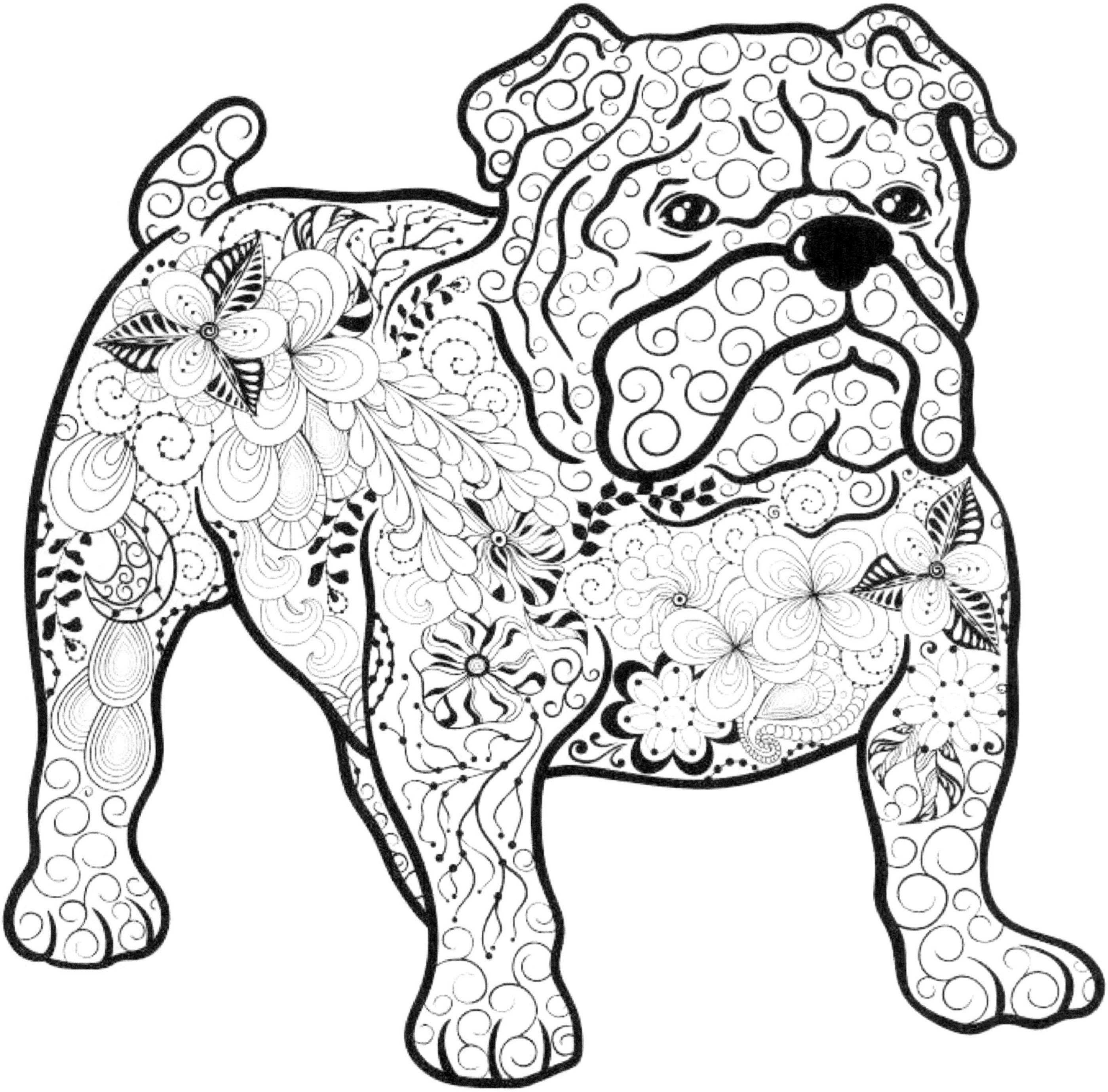

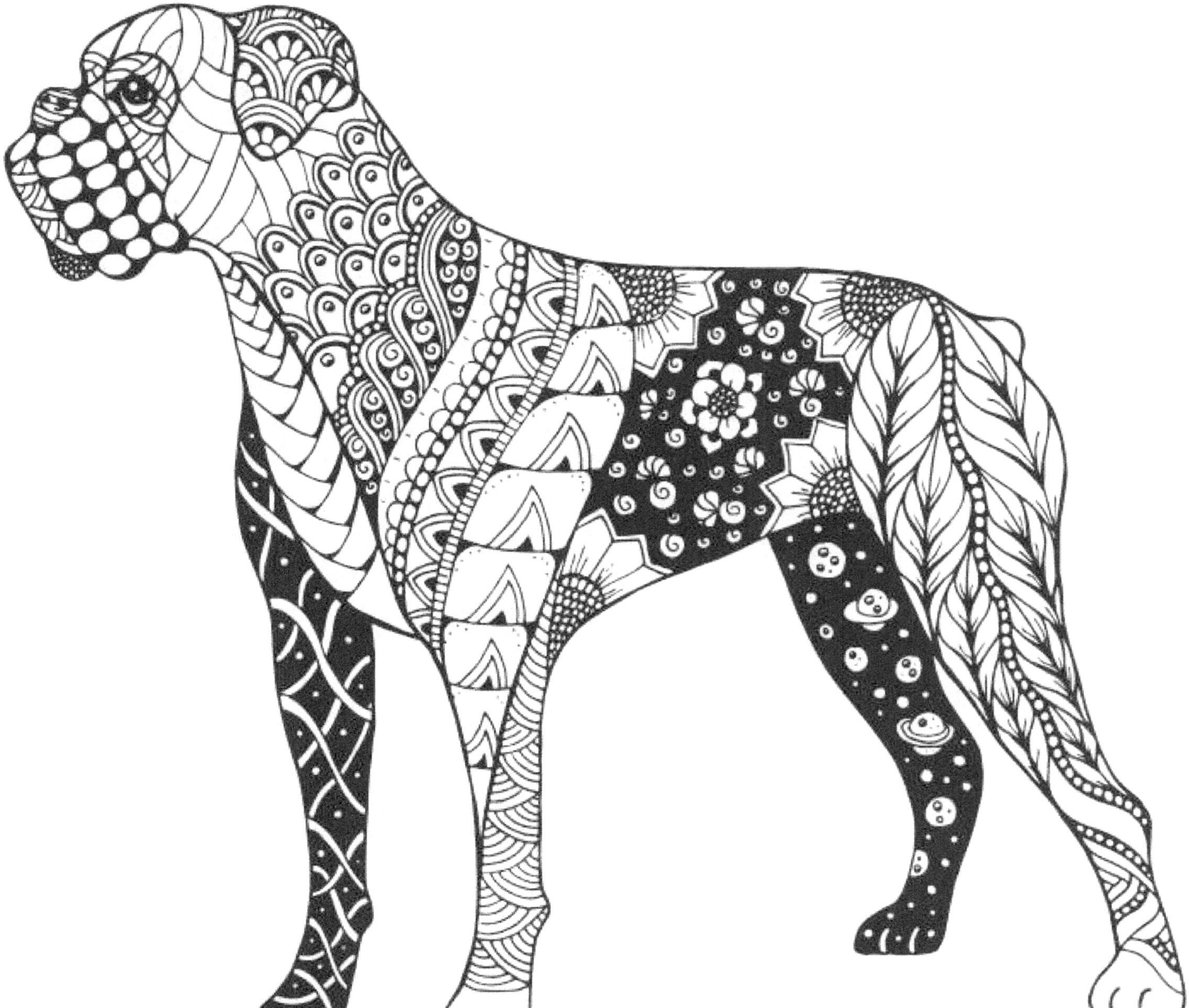

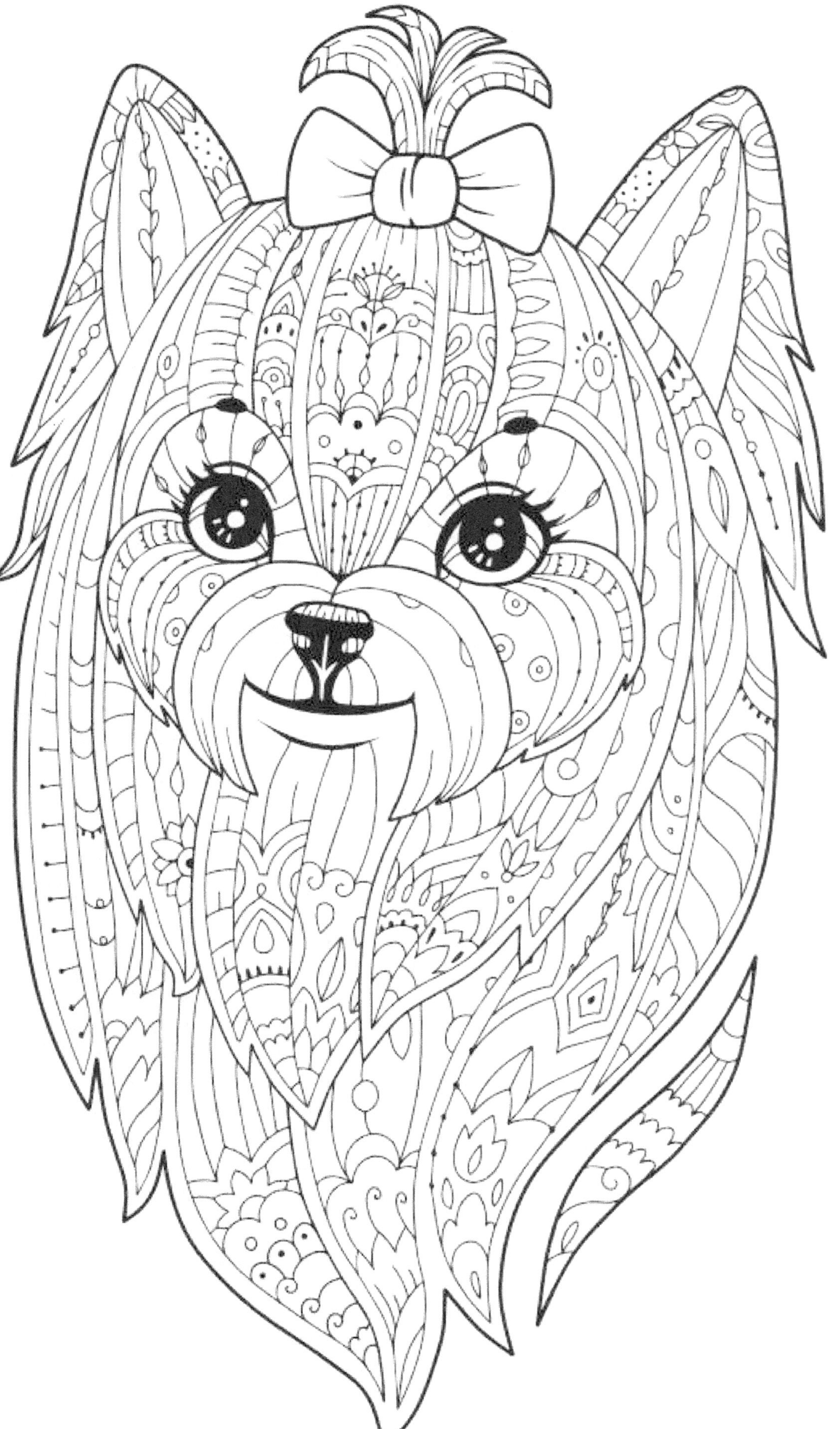

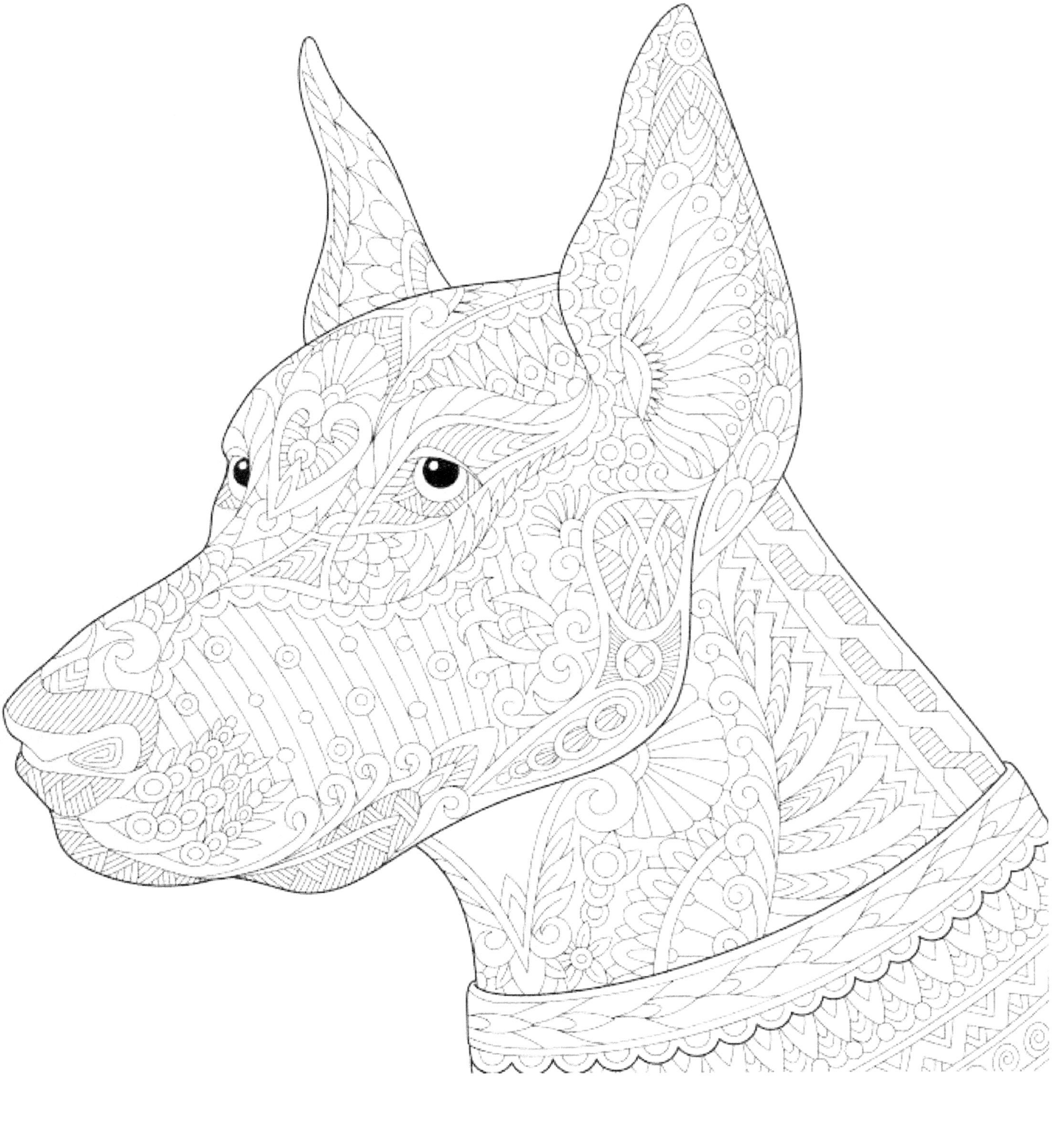

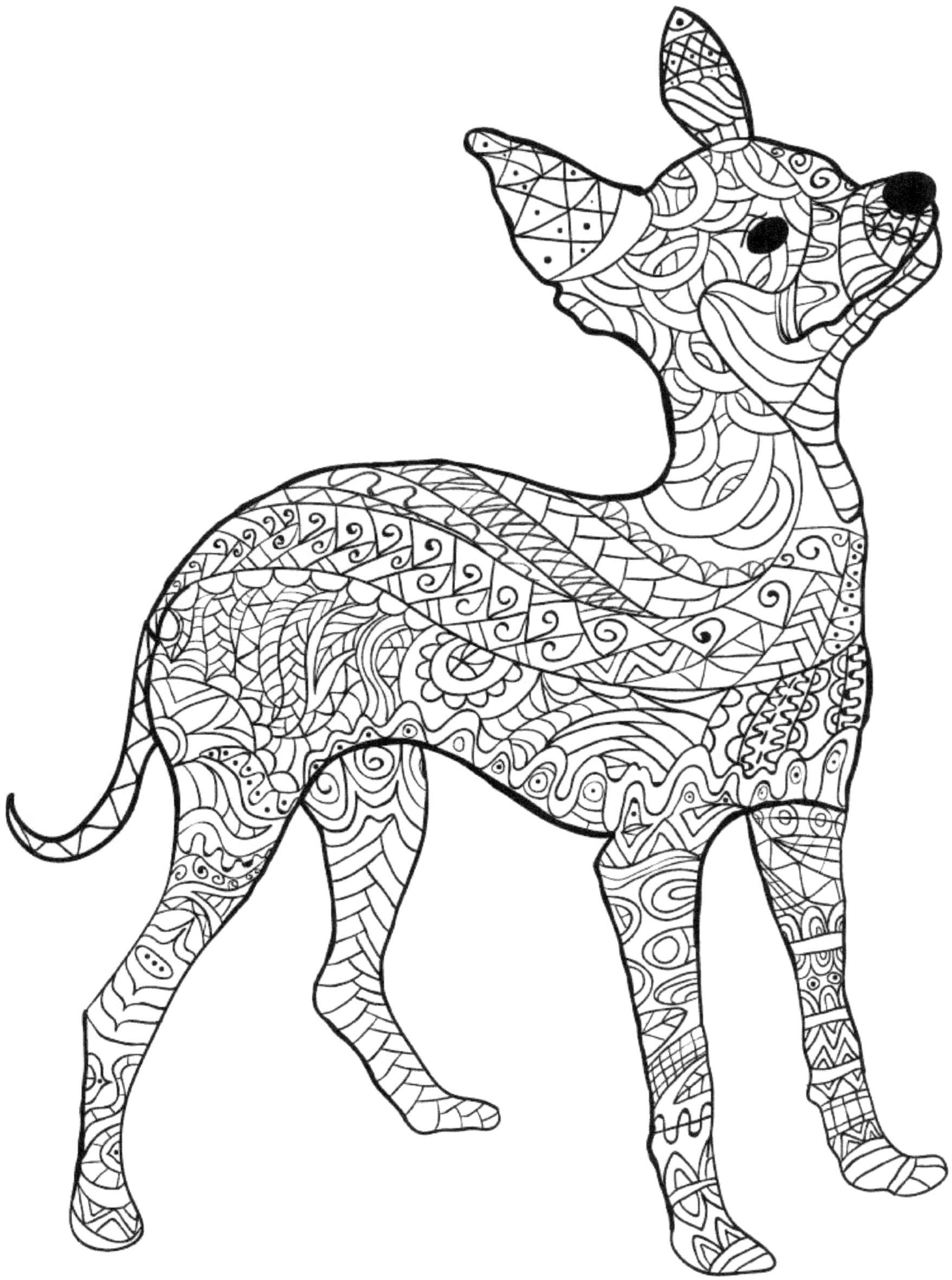

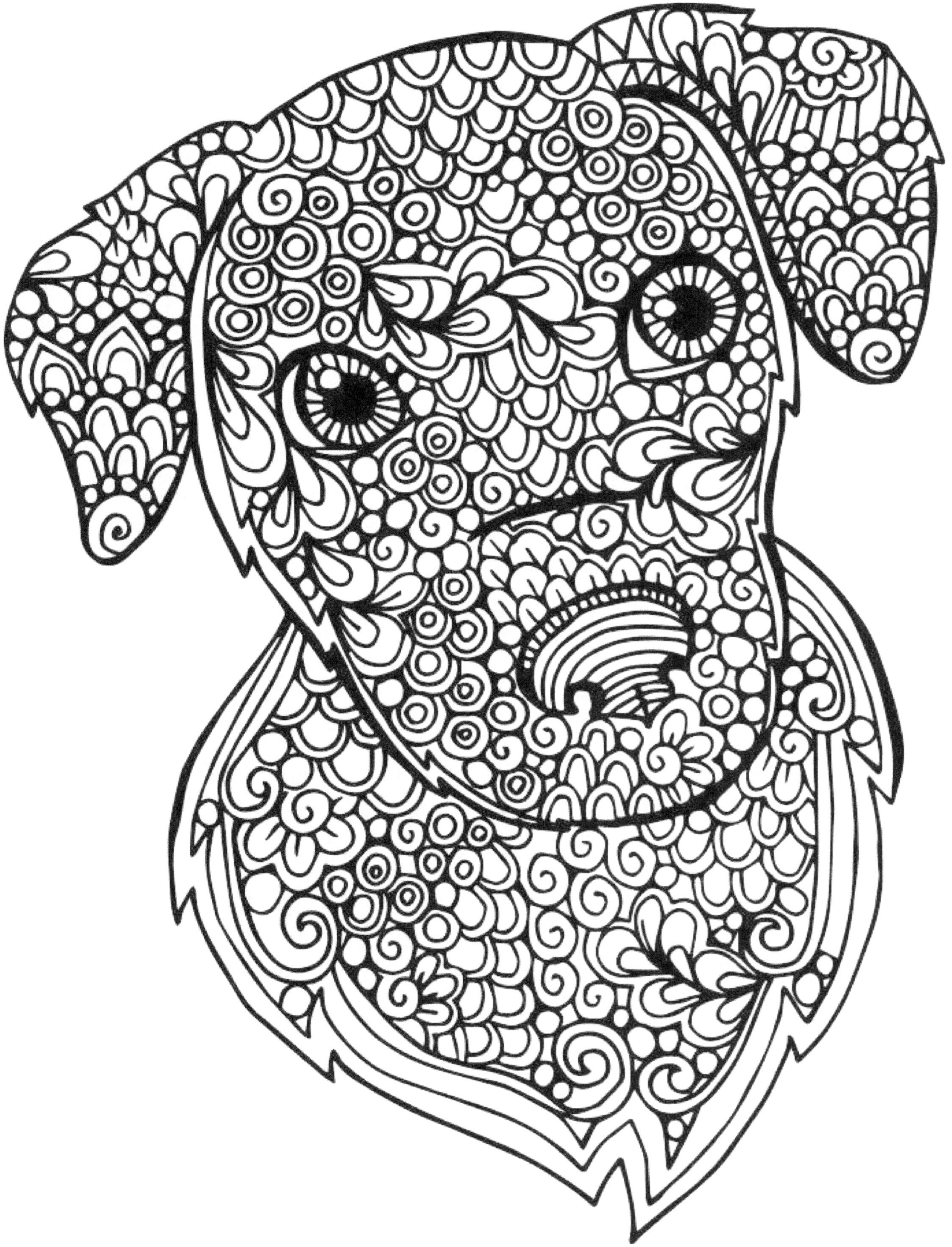

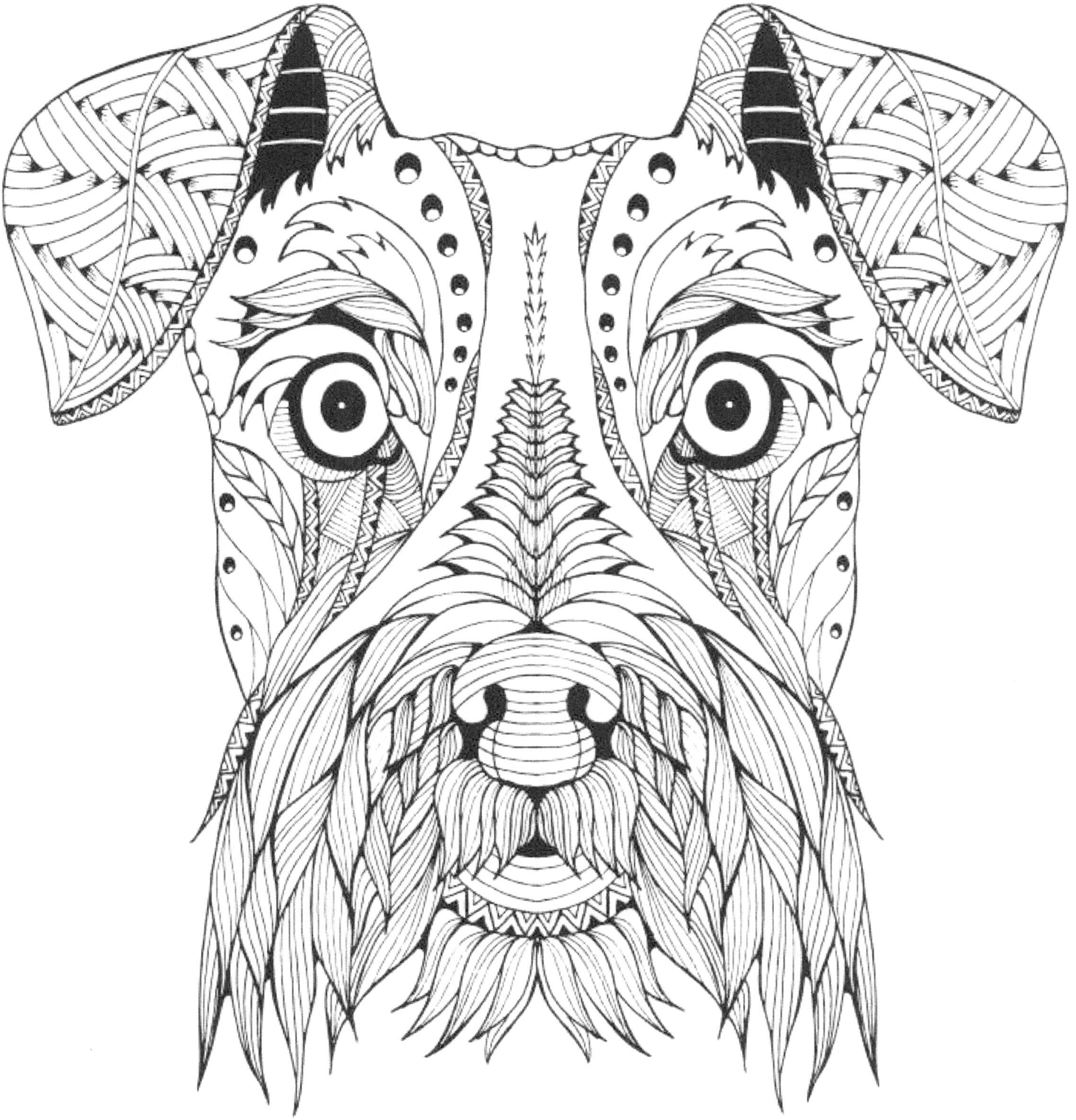

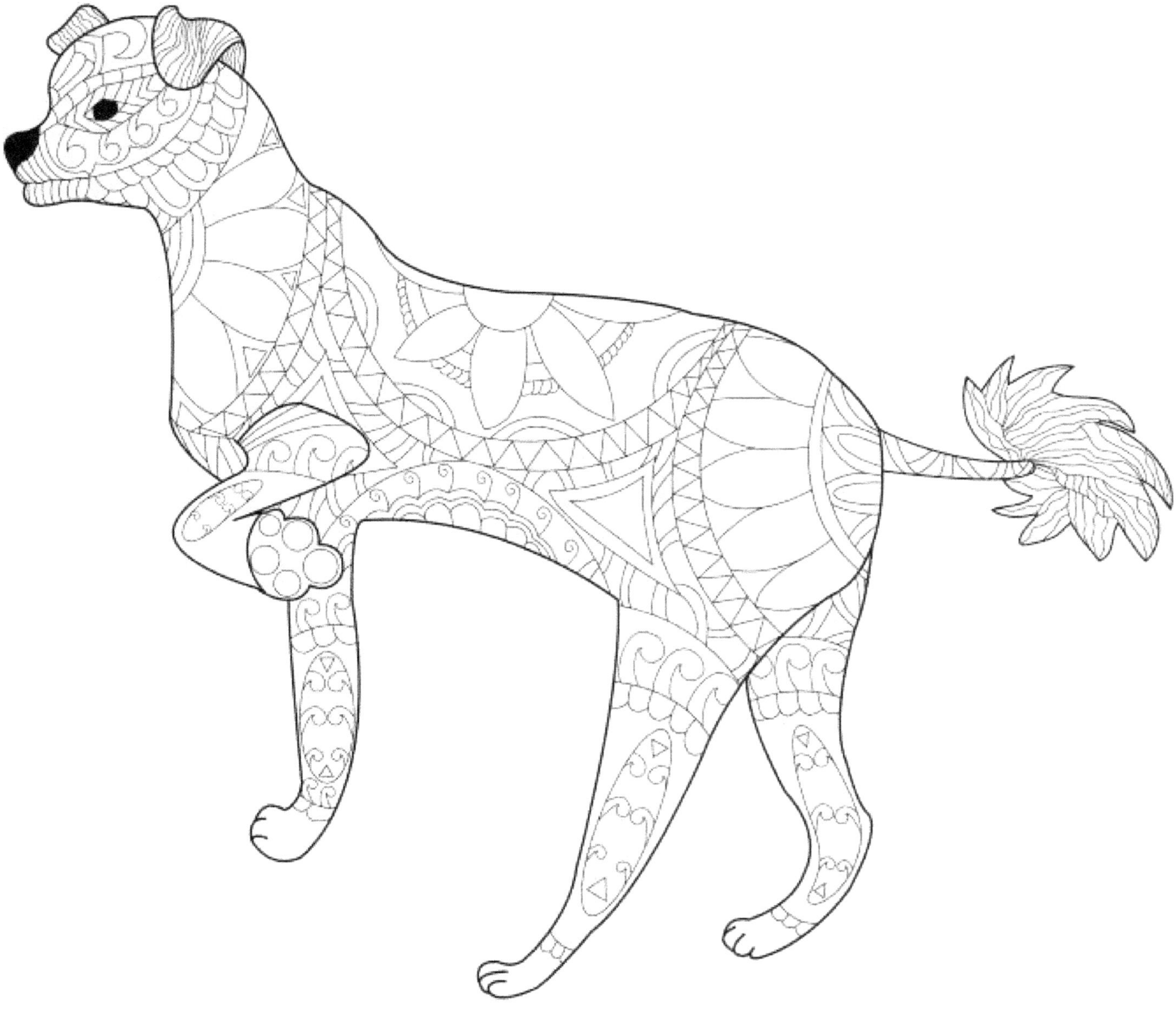

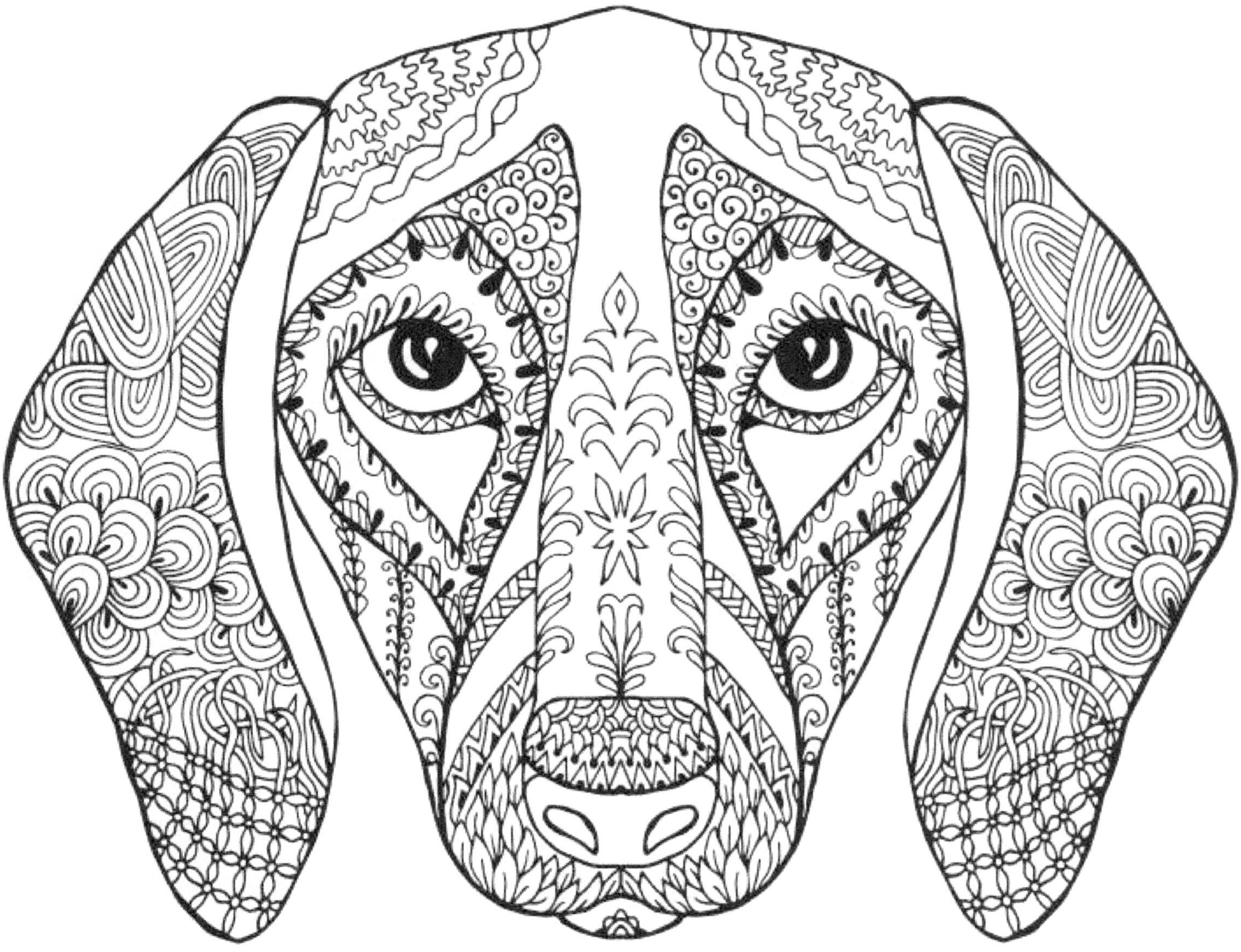

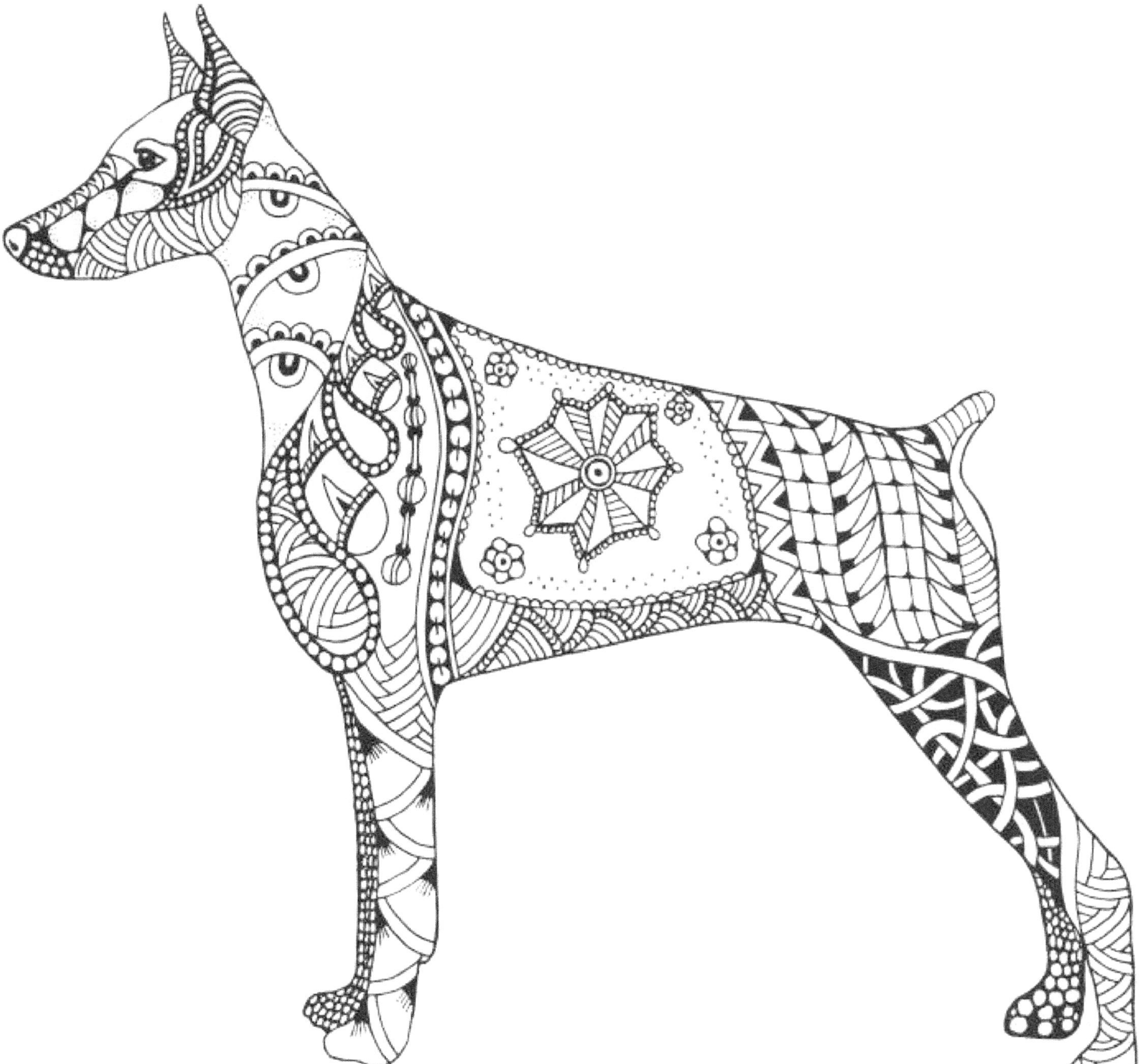

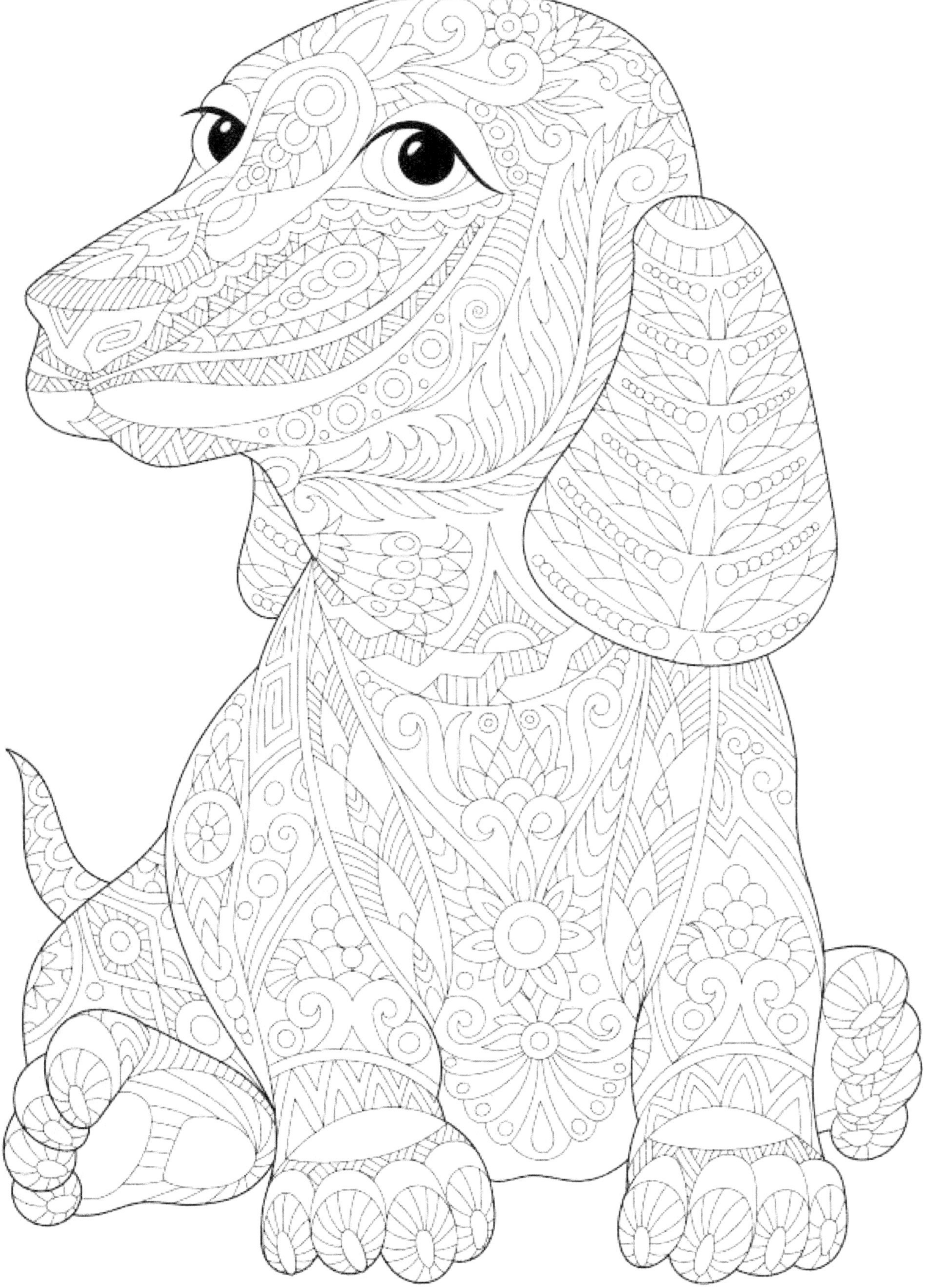

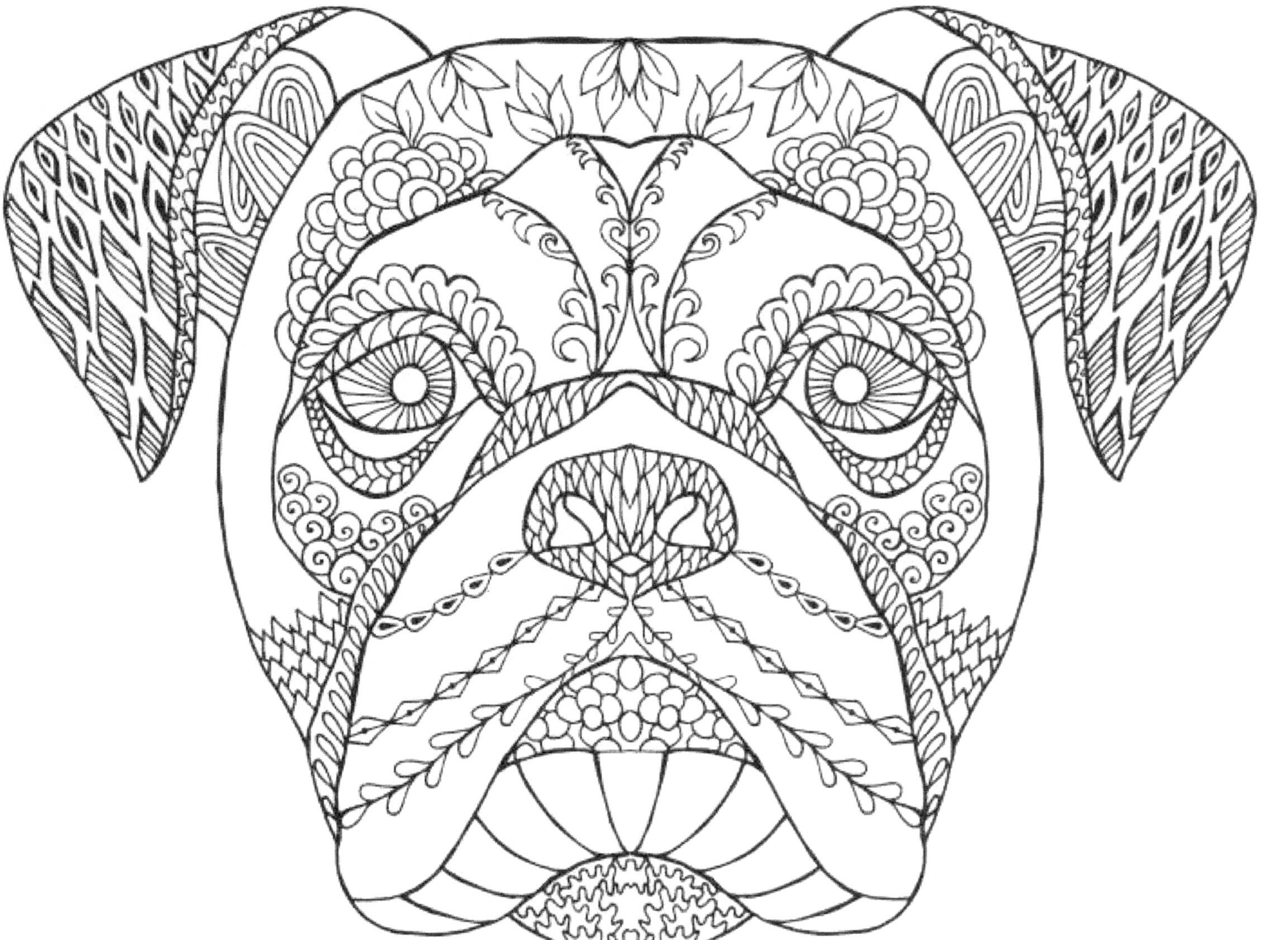

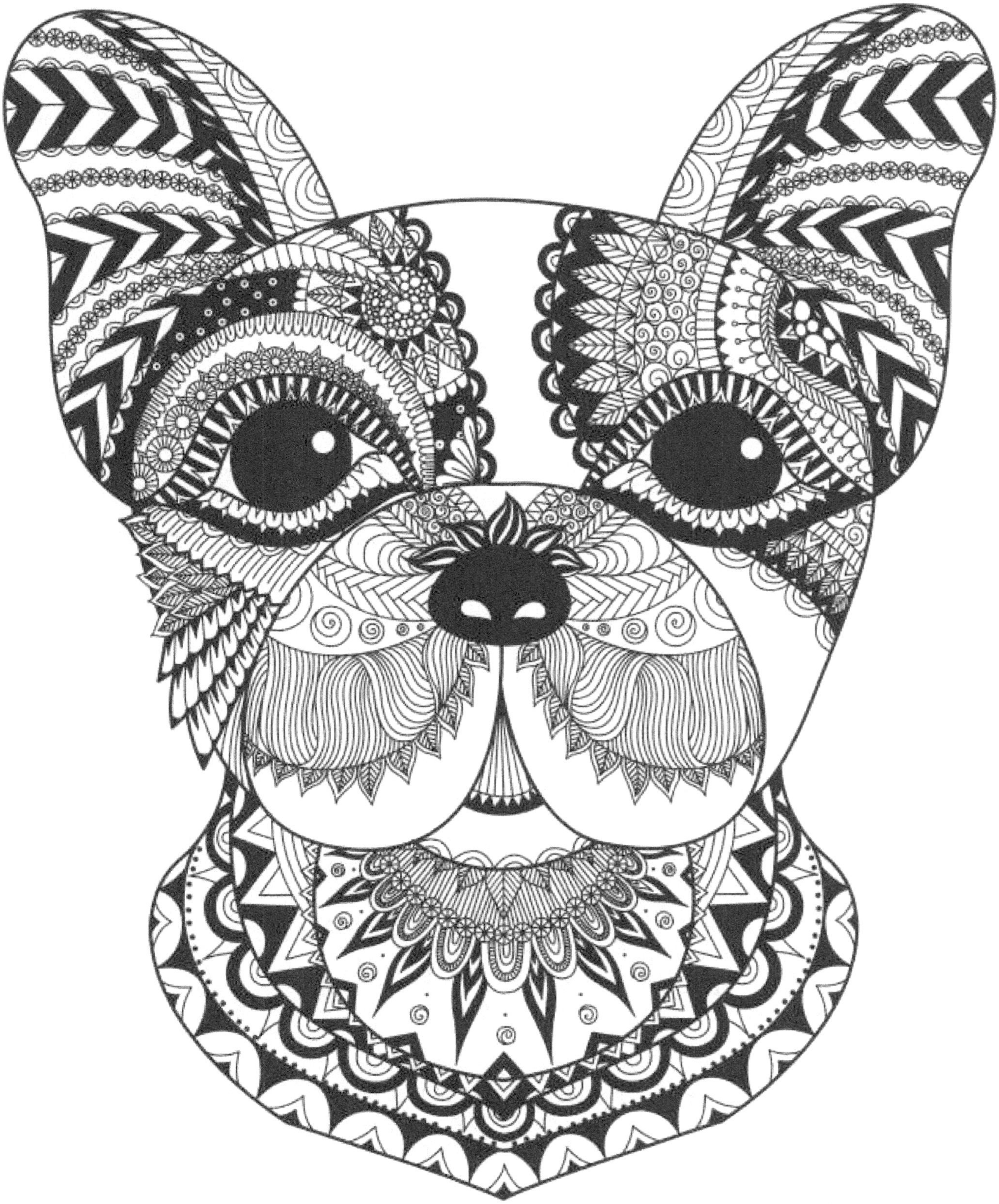

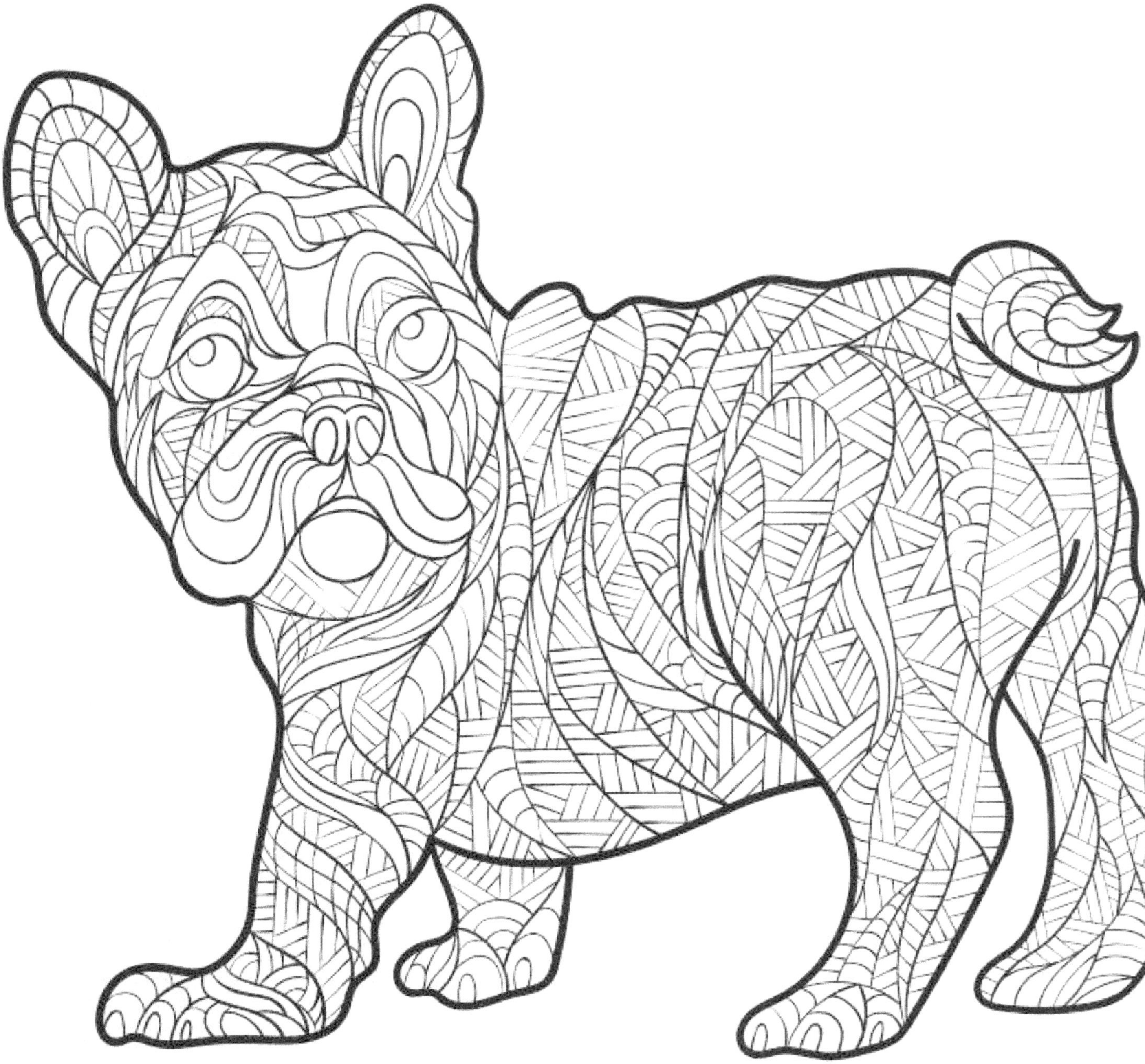

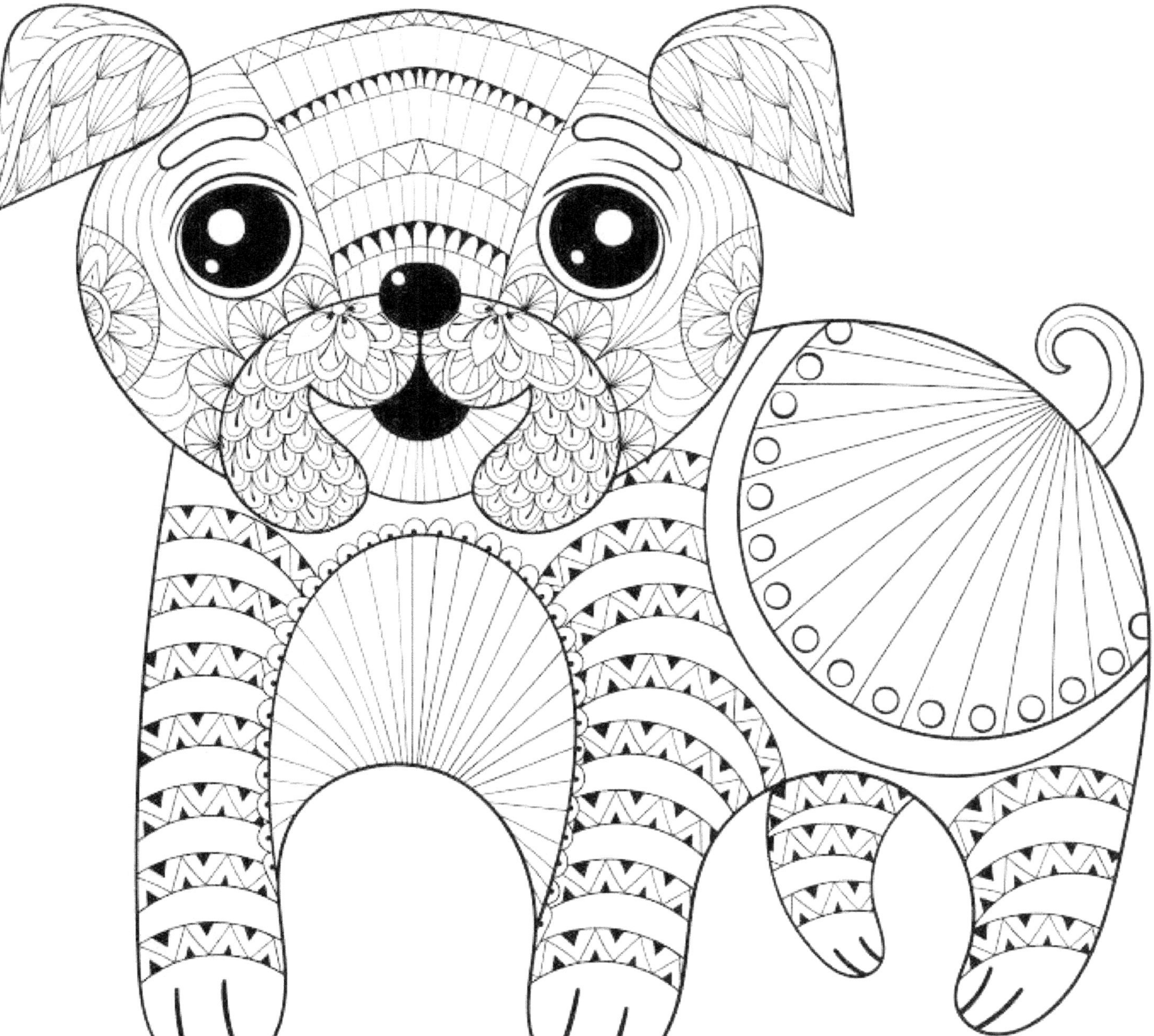

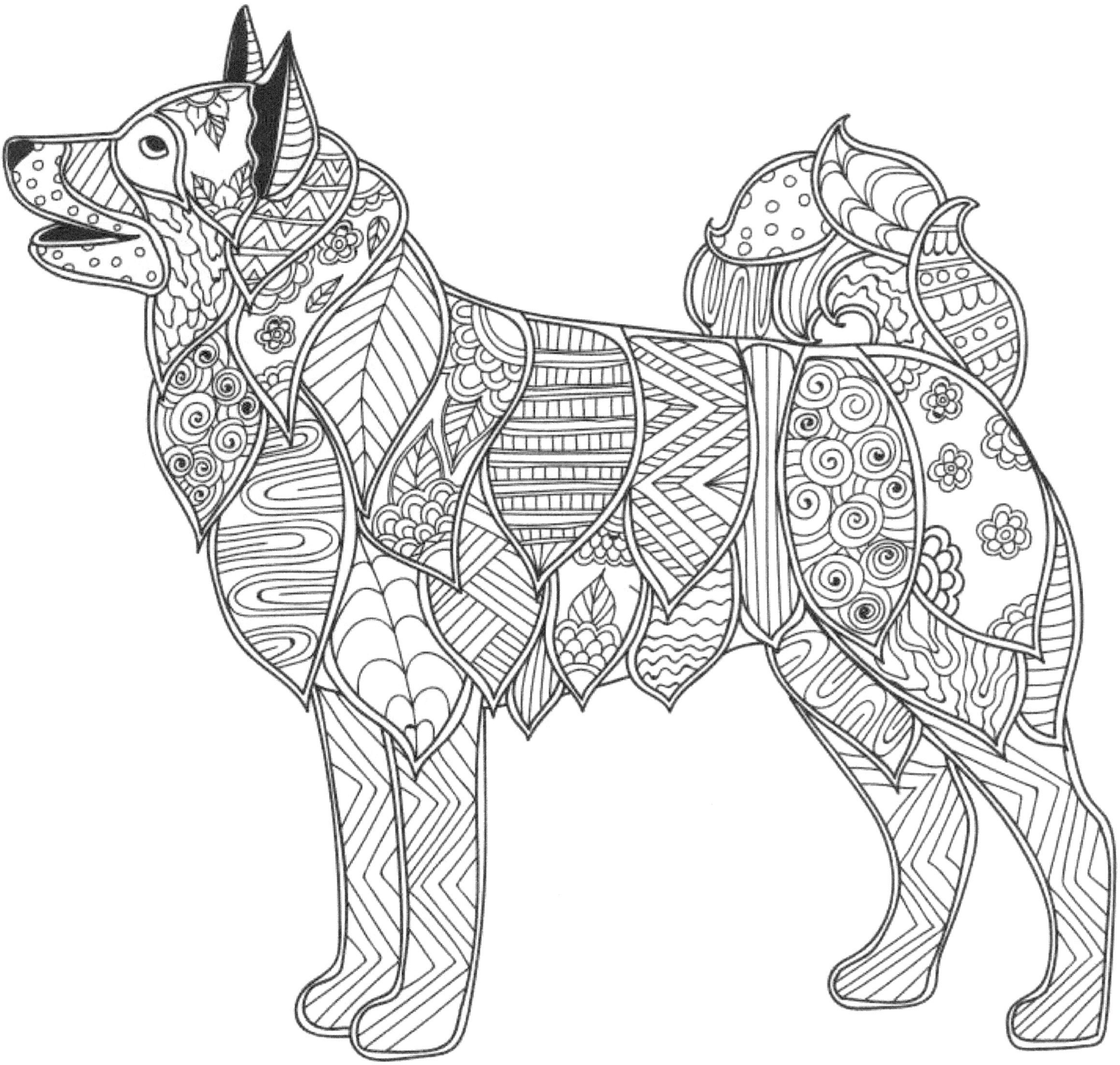

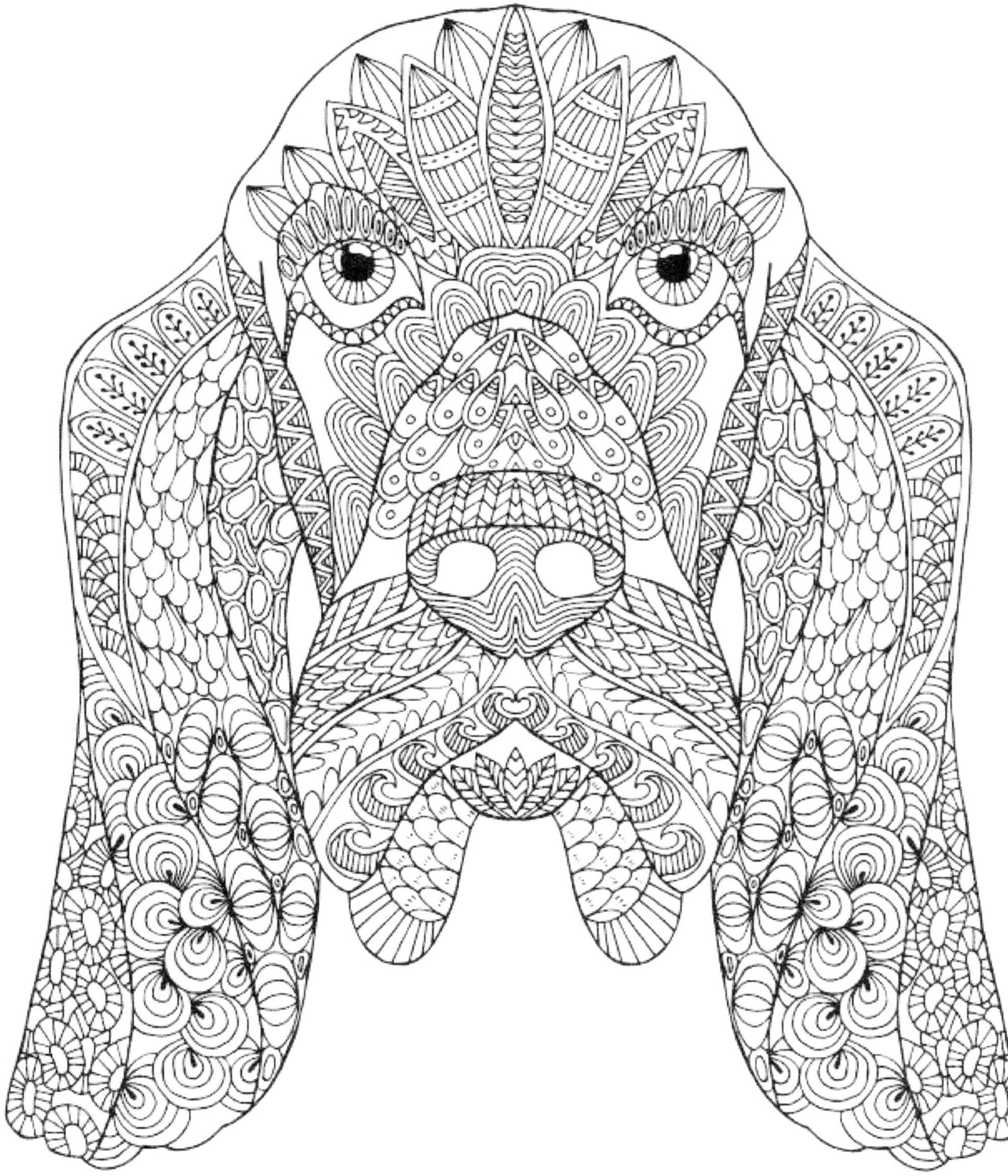

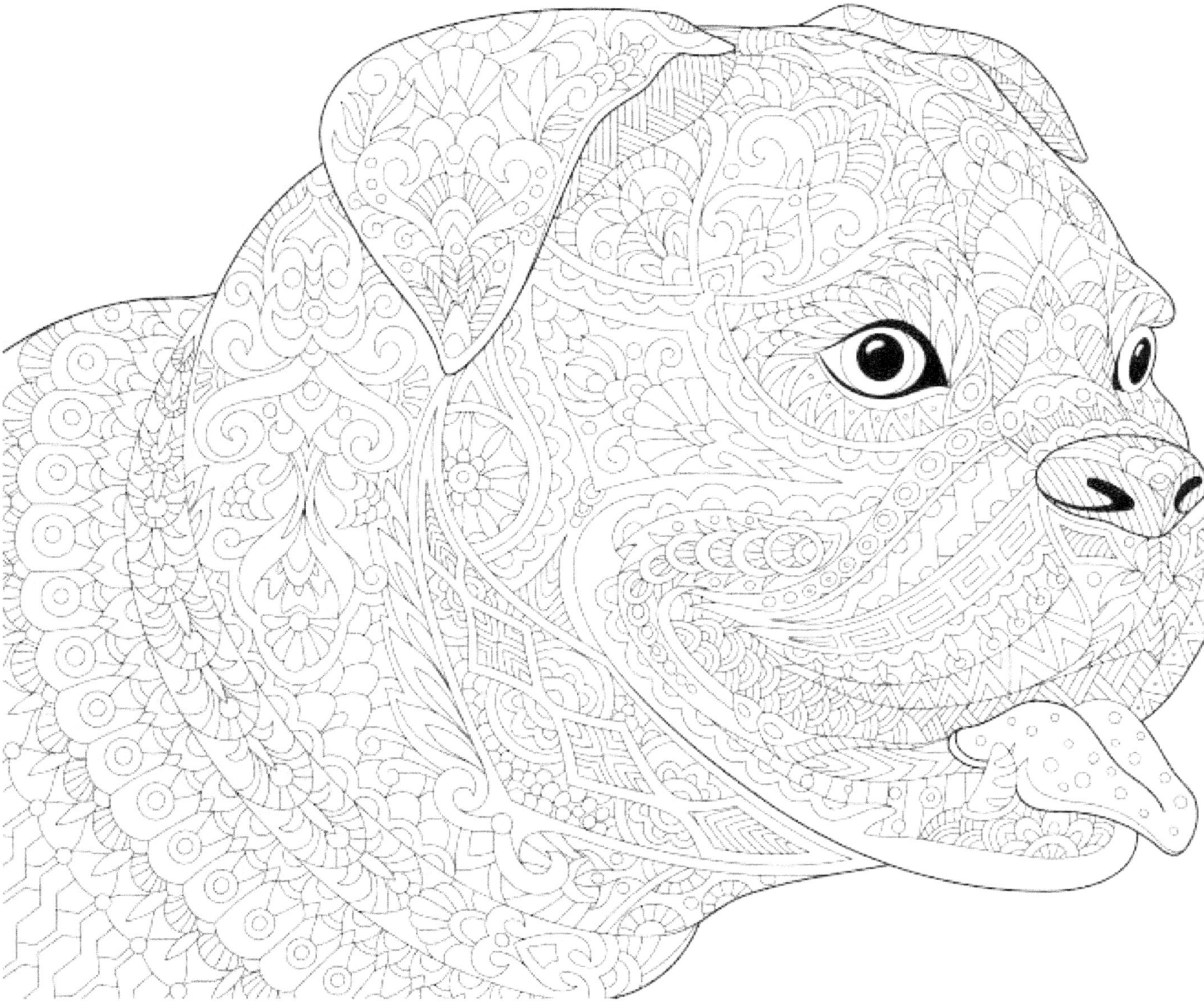

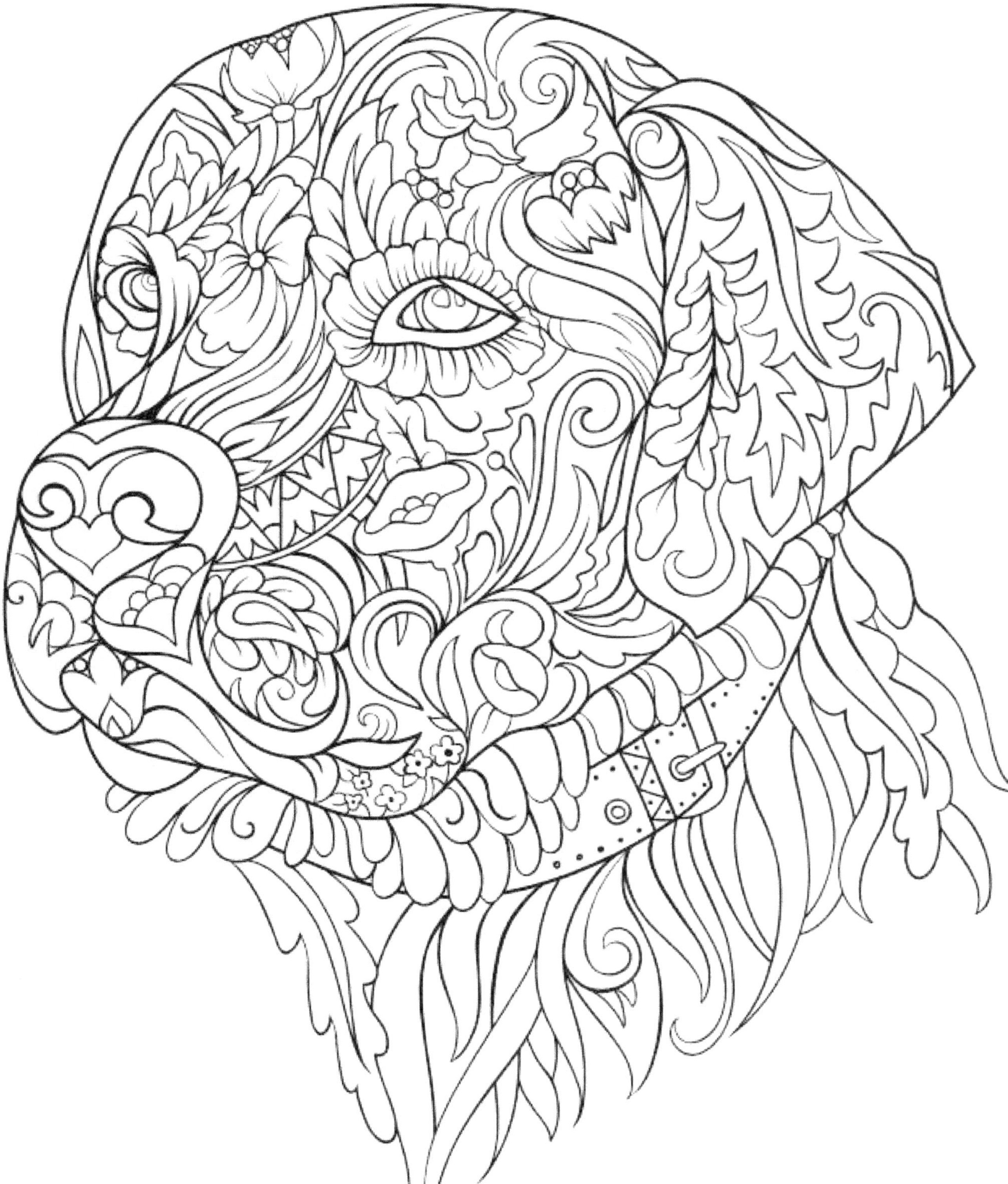

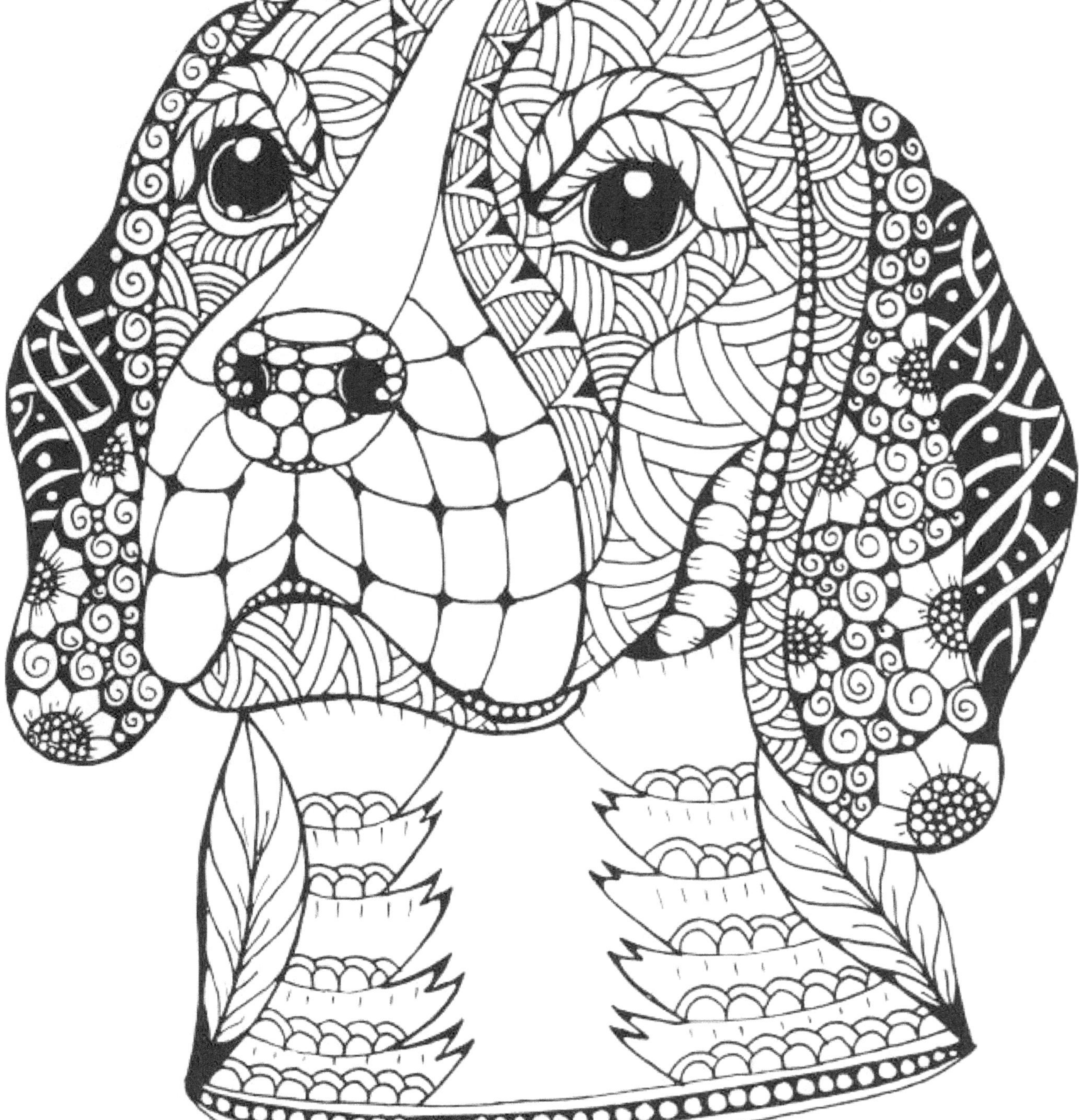

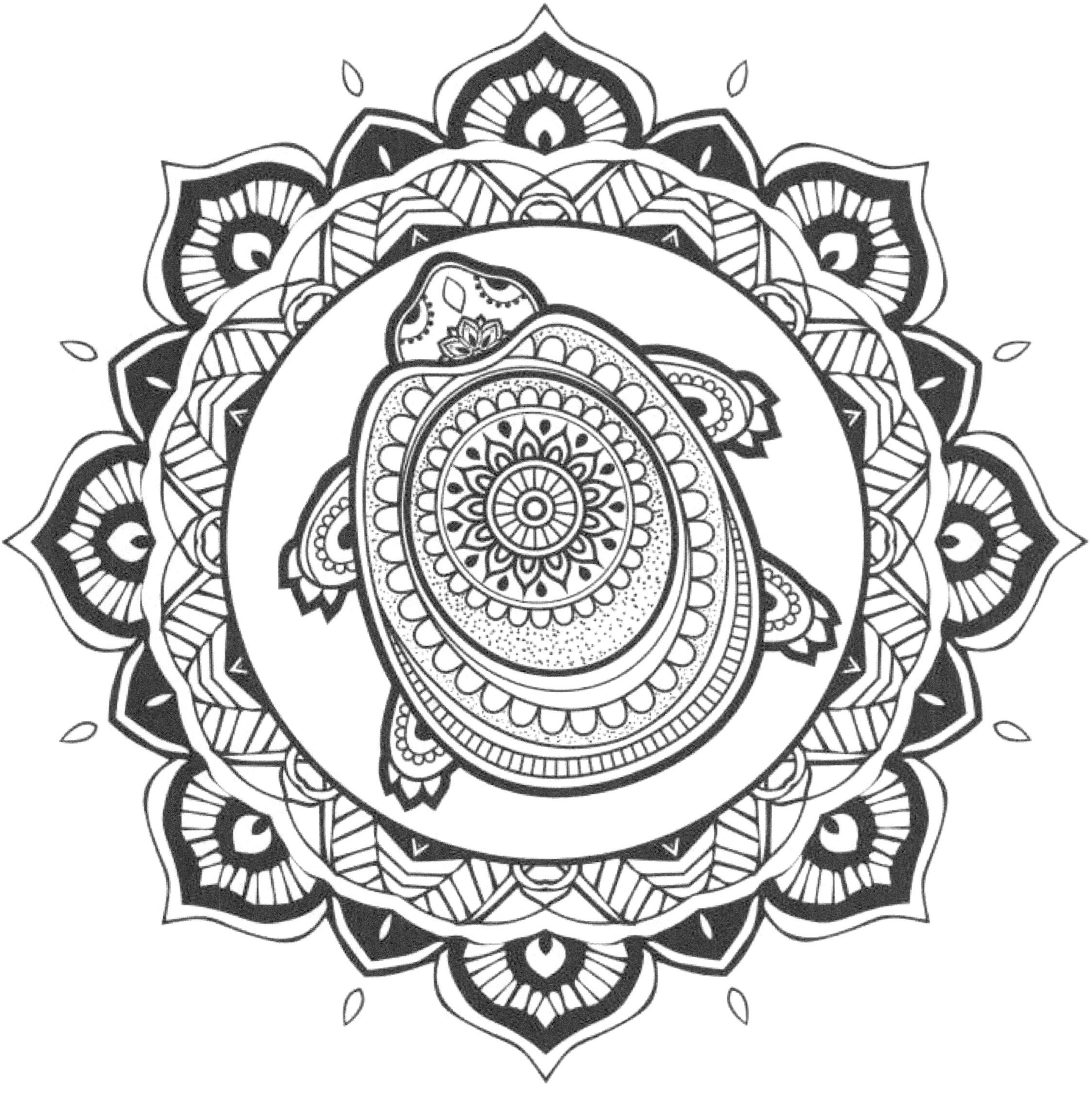

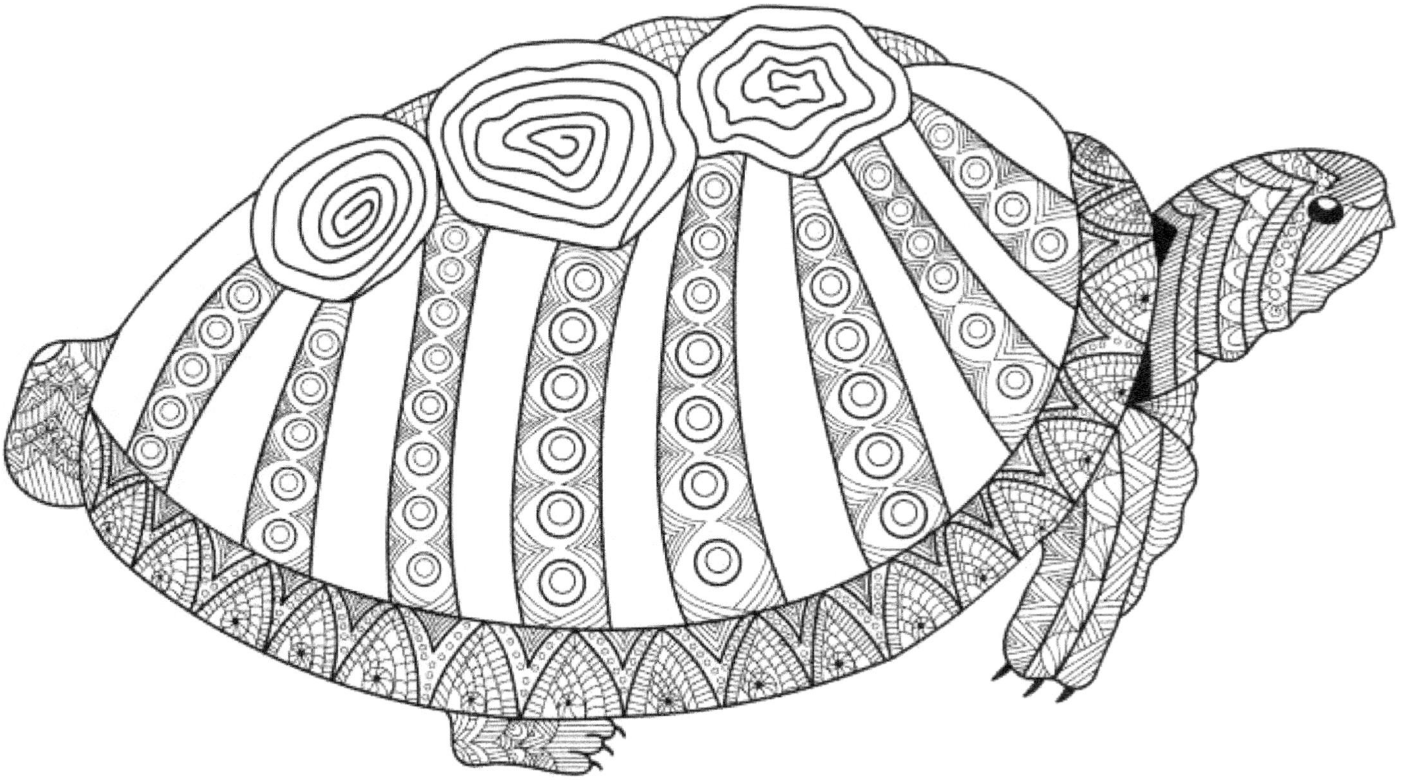

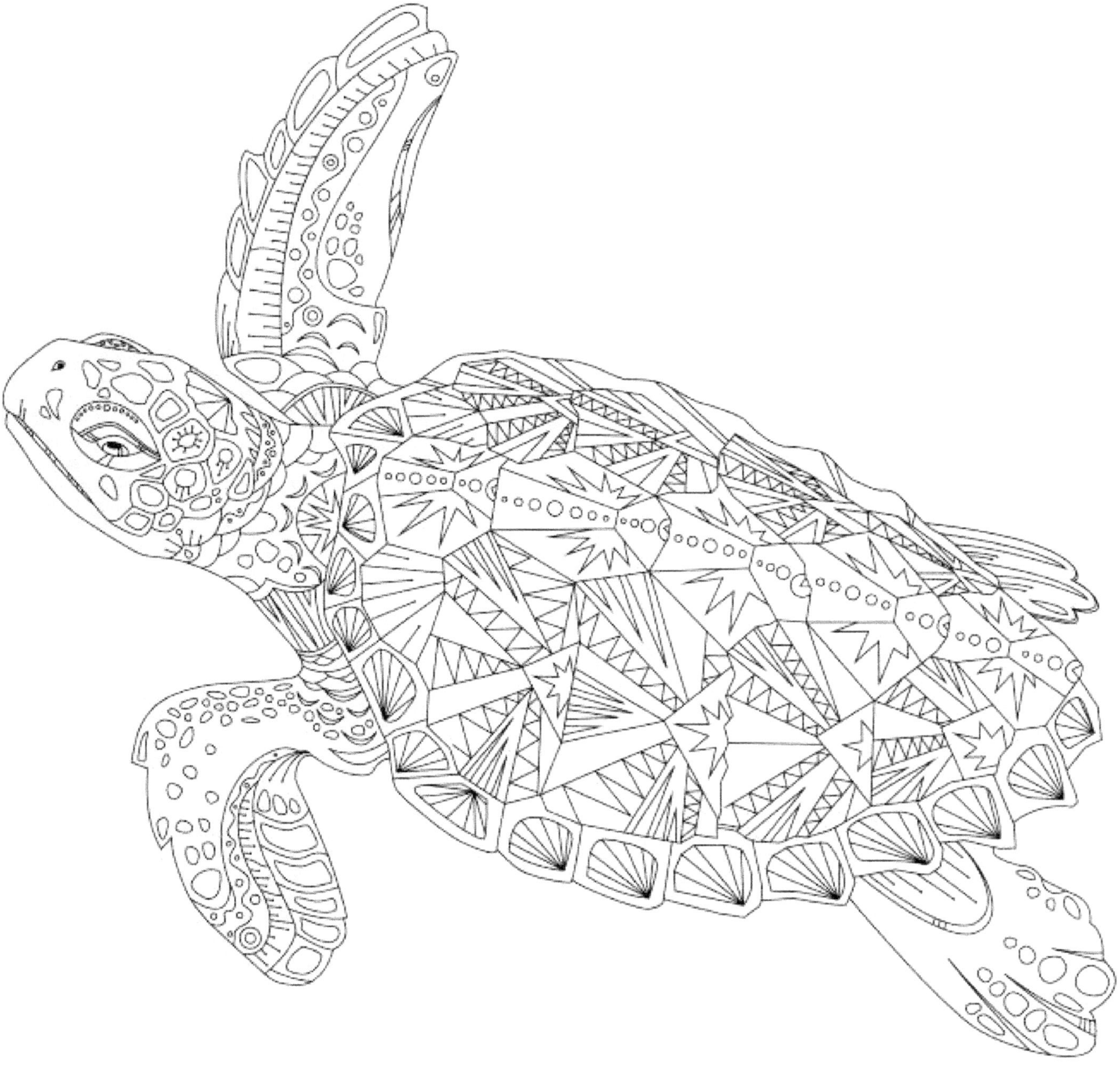

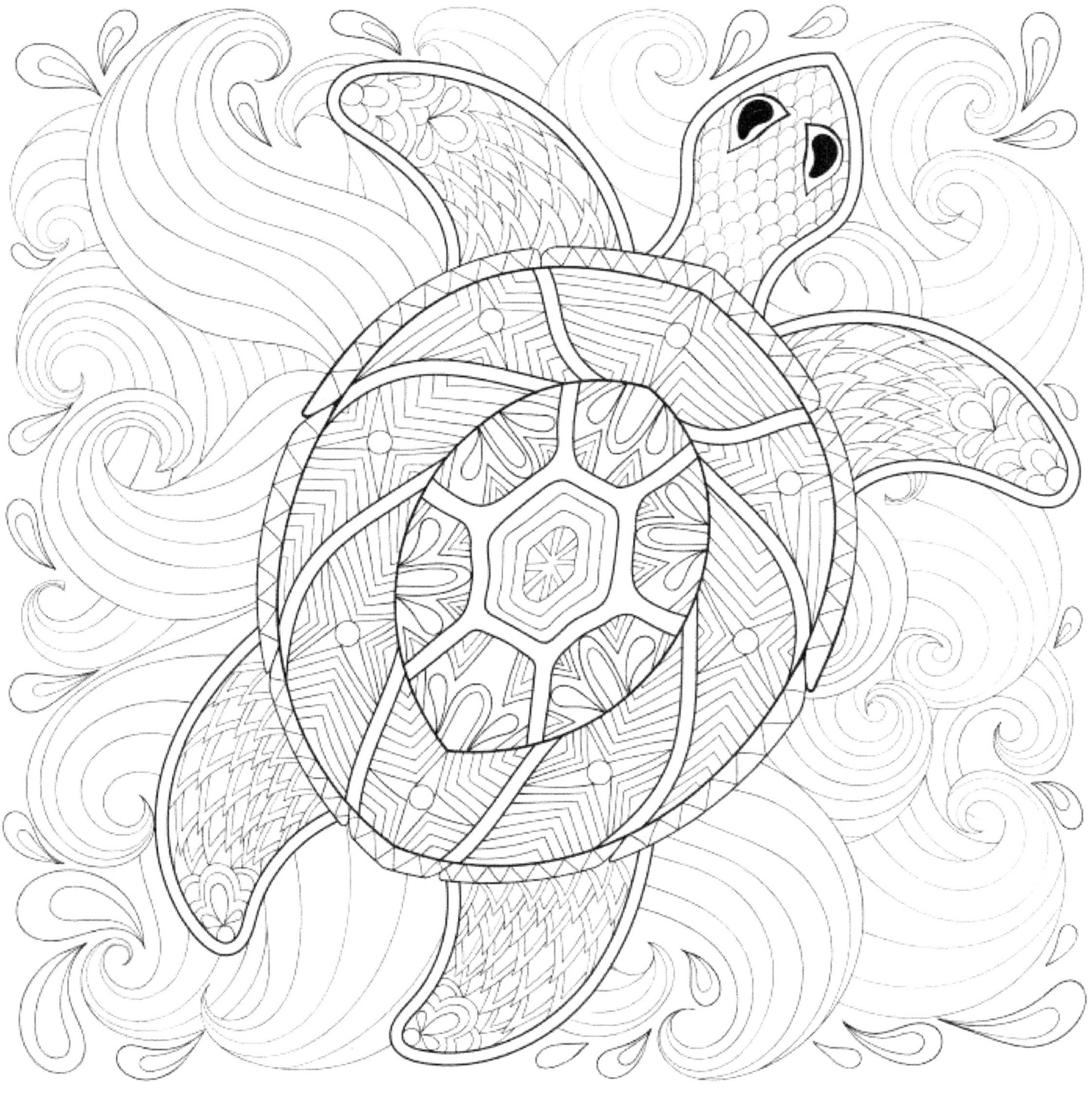

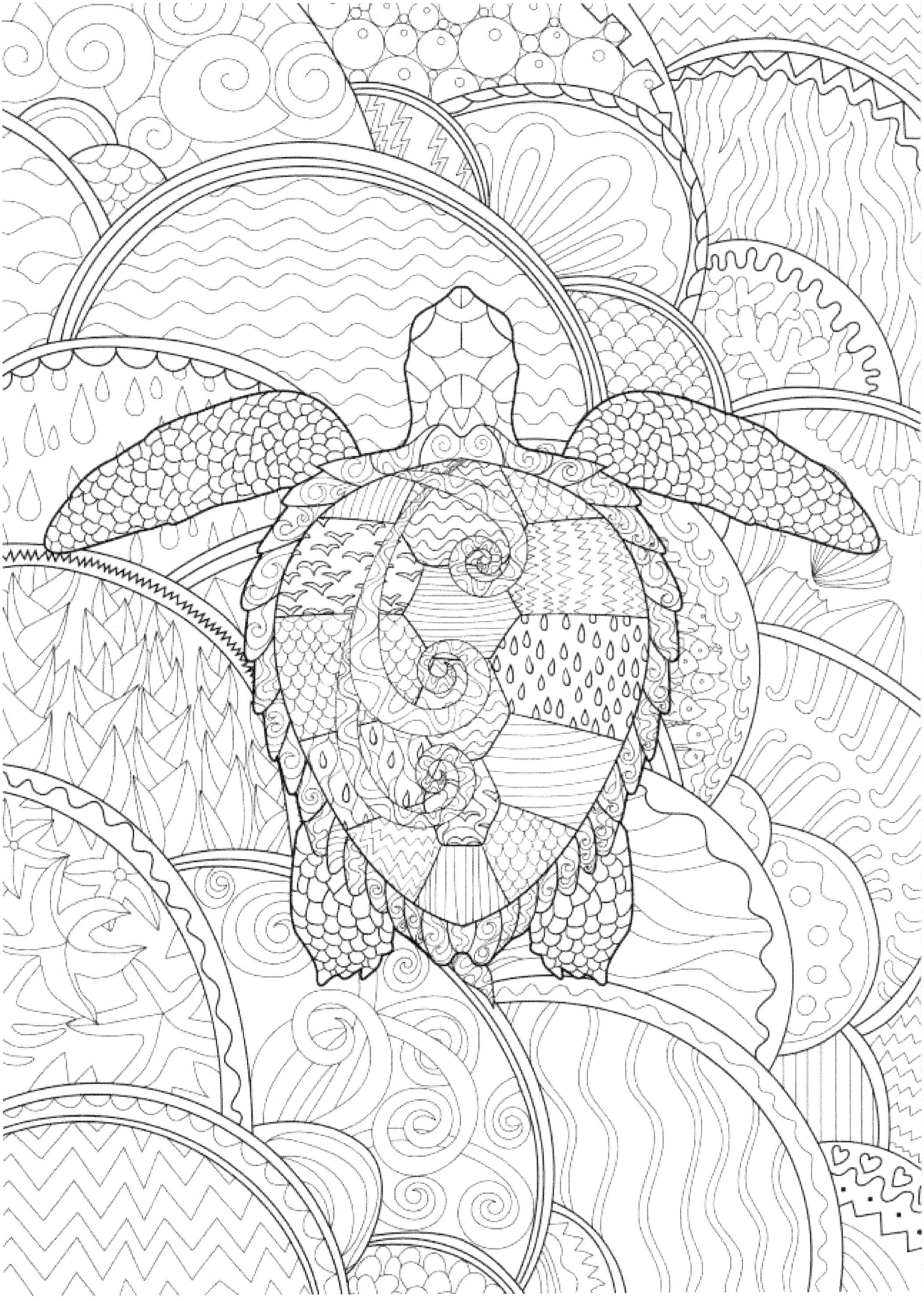

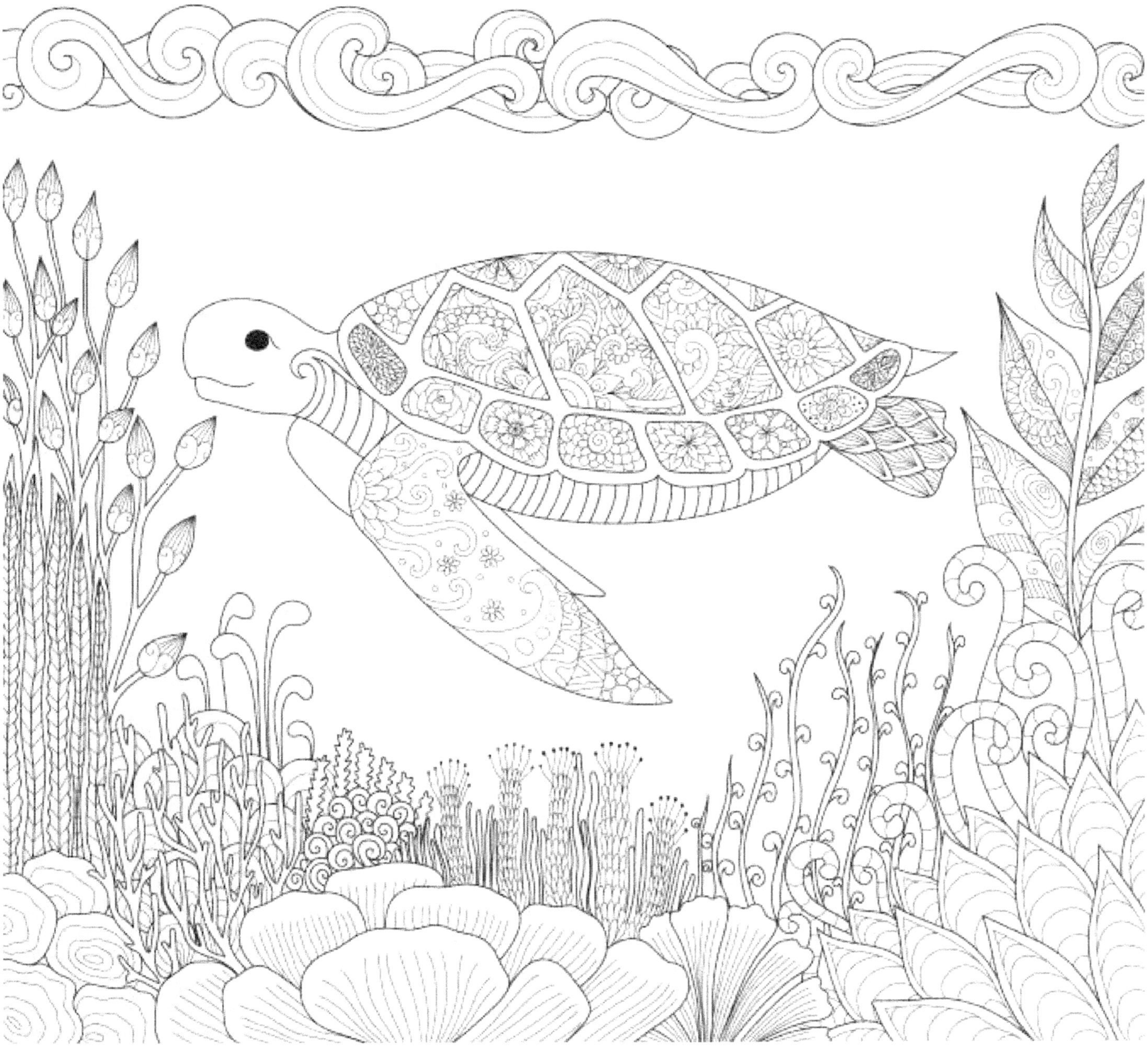

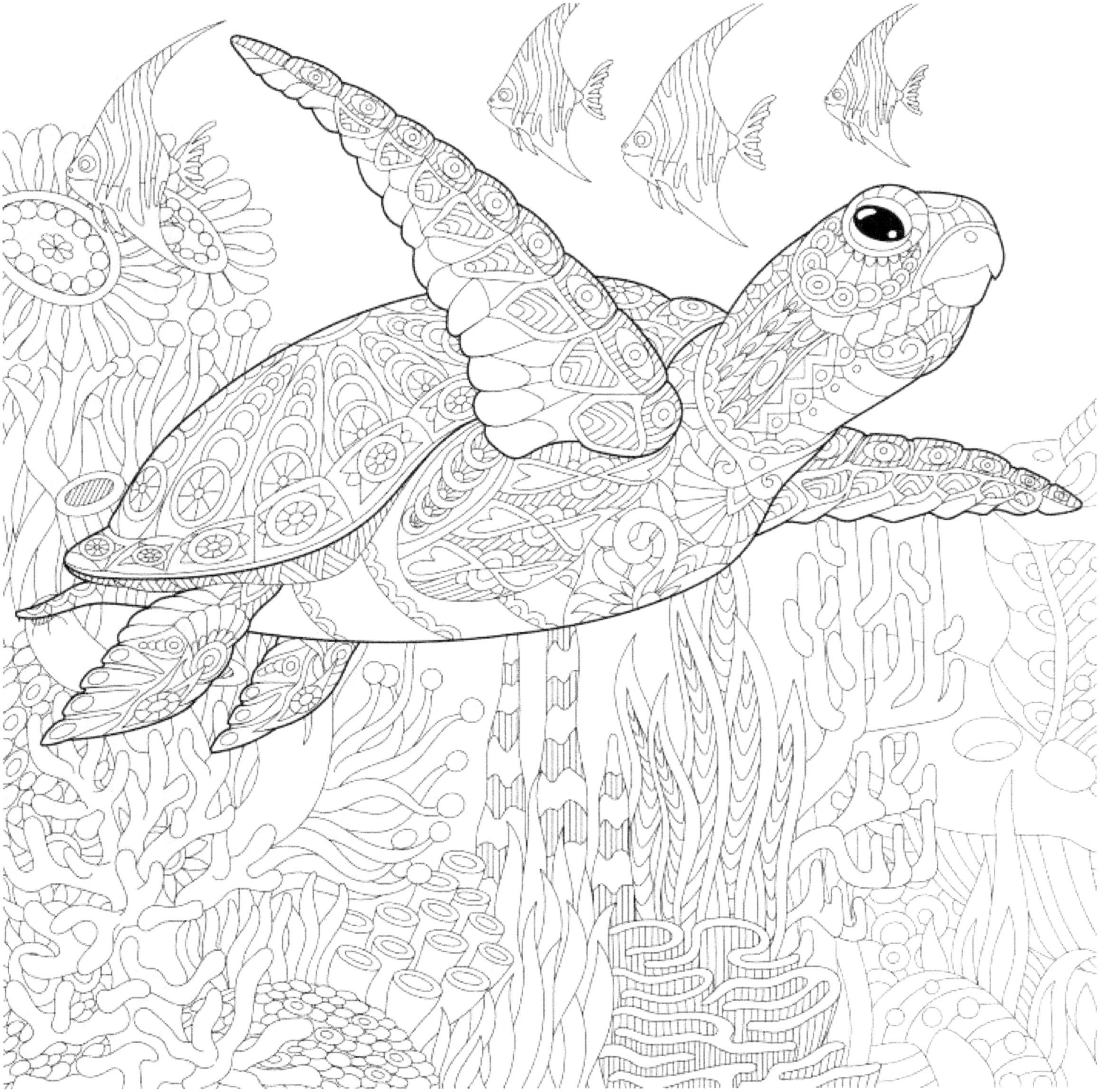

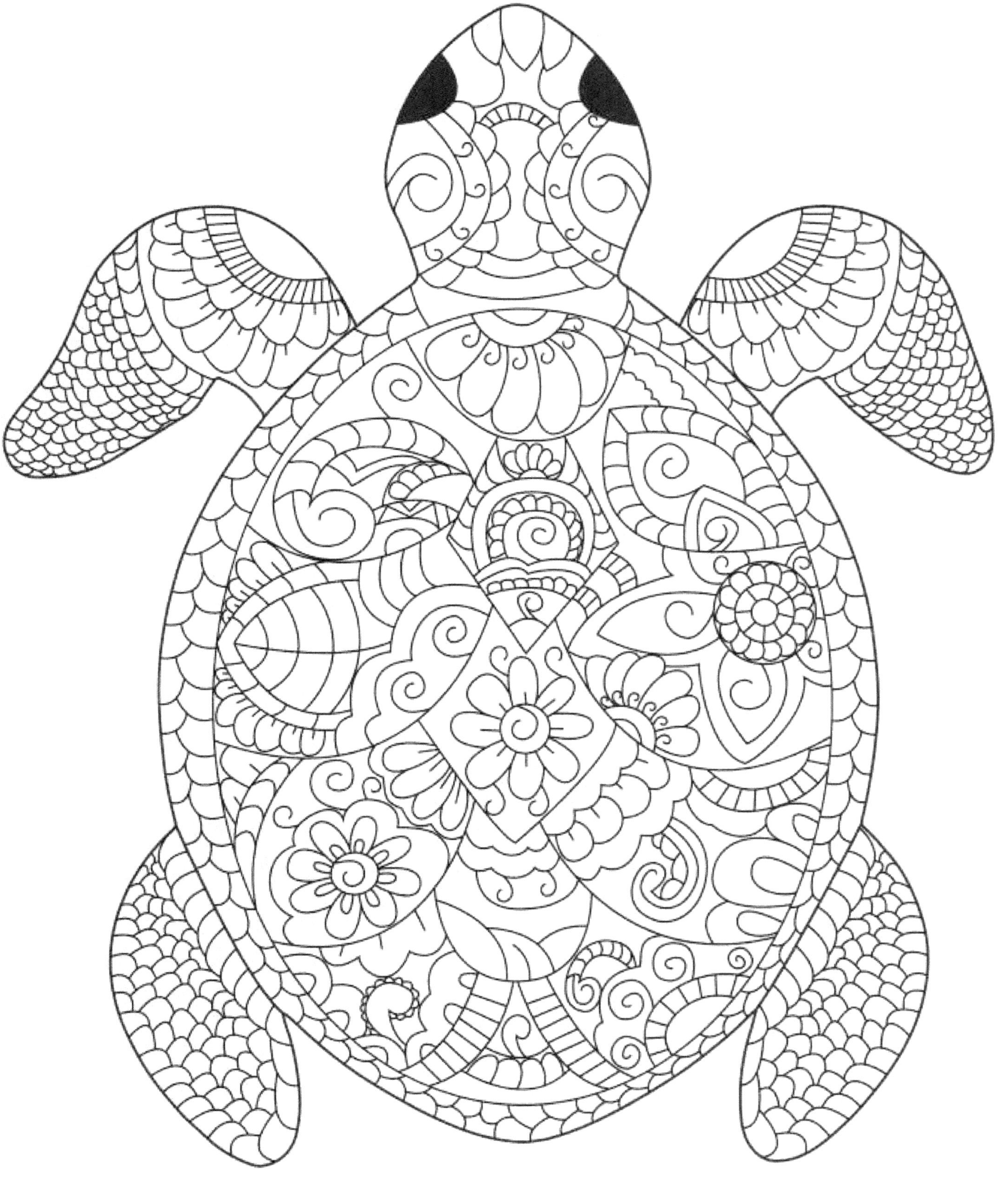

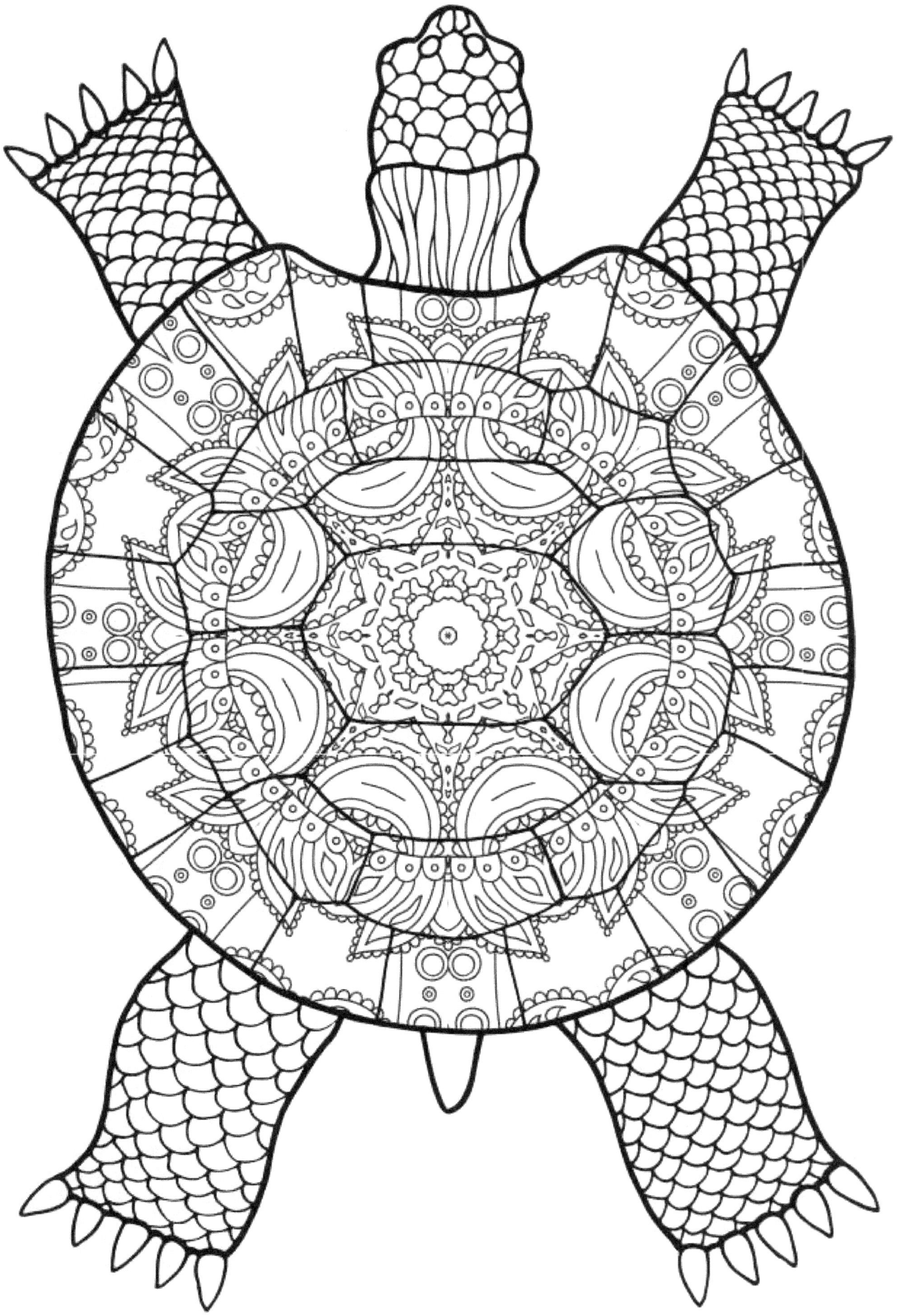

www.ingramcontent.com/pod-product-compliance
Lightning Source LLC
Chambersburg PA
CBHW081214170526
45165CB00009B/2817
* 9 7 8 1 5 4 8 2 1 6 9 0 0 *